ROMAN SPAIN

An introduction to the Roman antiquities of Spain and Portugal

by

F. J. WISEMAN, M.A.

LON[illegible]
G. BELL AND SONS, [illegible]
1956

TO

W. M. AND J. H. TENNANT

WHOSE LOVE OF SPAIN

PROVED SO INFECTIOUS

Printed in Great Britain by
The Camelot Press Ltd., London and Southampton

Preface

ALTHOUGH it is hoped that this book will prove acceptable to students of Latin, it has primarily been written for those whose interest in Spain is greater than their interest in Rome. To this end, therefore, Roman technical terms have been cut to a minimum, and where they have proved inevitable they should in their contexts be understandable. No doubt, too, there are over-simplifications perpetrated in the presumed interests of clarity. Roman place-names have in all necessary instances been carefully identified by their modern Spanish equivalents. Dimensions of buildings, etc., are given in English terms of yards and feet, but distances between one place and another are given in kilometres. The review of existing Roman monuments is preceded by a comprehensive chapter explaining the nature and functions of such buildings, but only in so far as they are found inside the Iberian Peninsula, including modern Portugal. The review itself is but an introduction to a vast subject with endless ramifications. In each province of modern Spain there are literally hundreds of Roman sites, large and small, and I do not claim that my treatment of even the larger ones is exhaustive.

I would like, finally, to acknowledge my indebtedness to many people: to my wife, who has accompanied me on my Spanish travels and also performed the major task of preparing the text for the publishers; to Mr. J. M. Biggins and his staff of the York Public

Reference Library for their unfailing courtesy and readiness to place at my disposal the many volumes I wished to consult; to Canon G. W. O. Addleshaw for guiding me to sources of information on the early history of the Western Church, which I might otherwise never have found—he should not, however, be held responsible for any misuse I may have made of these sources; to Dr. J. C. Serra-Rafols of Barcelona for a deal of stop-press news of Roman Spain; and to the Direccion General de Turismo in Madrid for so very kindly furnishing me with many of the photographs in this book.

F. J. WISEMAN

YORK
June 1955

Contents

PLANS

Plates

CHAPTER I

Rome and Carthage

IT was towards the end of the third century B.C. that Spain began to pass within the orbit of Rome at a particularly critical time in the latter's history: the decisive stage that had set Rome on the way to becoming a world power was already passed with the conquest of central and southern Italy, a long and laborious process that occupied most, if not all, of the two hundred years before 270 B.C., but one that was started almost accidentally, certainly without any conscious designs of empire. The factors that caused a small country town in the centre of Italy eventually to become the capital of a world-wide empire are difficult, if not impossible, to define: good fortune must certainly be numbered among them, for good fortune it was indeed, that she should be ready so precisely in time and place to be heir to the ramshackle empire of Alexander the Great and to fill so rapidly the vacuum caused by his extravagant conquests: but before that could be, Rome had to fight the hardest and most searching war of her long history, the second war against Carthage.

Carthage had been founded in the recess of a large bay in the north of Tunis by Phoenician *émigrés* from Tyre in the ninth century: the exact site of the foundation has since been rendered unrecognisable by drifting sands: modern Carthage on its present site is of a later Roman origin. From the start the original Carthage was true to the traditions of her Semitic ancestors and made trade her main business; and this over the years made her pre-eminent in the Western Mediterranean, with strong commercial interests in Spain, particularly in the south. But before one quarter of the third century B.C. had run its course it was becoming obvious that Rome, expanding rapidly to the south of Italy as one conquest led willy-nilly to another, was a new power to be reckoned with; not, indeed, it was true, as a commercial rival, but as a force that was likely to remove customers, potential and real, by the simple process of swallowing them up: and to Carthaginian eyes, at least, there was no guarantee that this process would be confined to customers.

The absorption, therefore, into the Roman State of the Greek communities of the south of Italy led almost inevitably in the year 264 B.C. to the outbreak of war with Carthage—the First Punic War—and it ended in the year 241 B.C. in victory for the Romans: they did not win all the battles in it, but they were becoming adepts at winning the decisive one: steadiness and resoluteness in the face of adversity were not the least of the qualities that were destined to make them, in the end, masters of the known world.

One feels that it was at the end of this war that almost for the first time Rome began to be conscious of her strength: she now had Sicily to add to her conquests, which at this stage extended from there to the Po valley beyond the Appenines: she had emerged from the war as a power on the sea: if her initial improvisations on this element had been clumsy, they had at least been effective, but to the end of their days the Romans were always strangely ill at ease on the sea, in strong contrast to their Greek neighbours. Yet by that odd streak in human nature that makes a comedian want to play Hamlet, it may well have been this unexpected success on an element for which they had little aptitude, that began to go to their heads and caused them to adopt a somewhat contemptuous attitude towards their newly vanquished opponents, an attitude that before very long they were to have good reason to revise.

The first-fruits of this new mood were favourable: scarcely two years passed after the end of the war before Sardinia and Corsica fell into their lap, like ripe plums that had somehow, inexplicably, survived the first shaking of the tree. In the meantime the defeated Carthaginians were in the throes of a particularly bitter civil war, from which they were delivered after three years by the strong hand of a member of one of their leading families, Hamilcar Barca. Democracy of a sort traditionally existed in Carthage, but it lived in a kind of suspended animation, public opinion rarely asserting itself, and that, only at moments of national crisis: such an atmosphere was therefore favourable to the schemes of ambitious men, and if Hamilcar Barca received no enthusiastic support, he did at least meet with little opposition to his plans for revenge on Rome.

Consequently in 237 B.C. he crossed with an armed force to Spain to restore the position previously enjoyed there by the Carthaginians. For one of the consequences of losing the war against Rome had been the almost complete obliteration of Carthaginian influence in Spain. Landing at Cadiz, he quickly regained control of the southern coast and was busy working his way up the east coast when further progress was arrested by the accident of his death by drowning in the river Vinalapo at Elche (20 kms. from Alicante) in the year 227 B.C. His successor was Hasdrubal, his son-in-law, hand-picked for the job. Under his vigorous direction Carthaginian arms were advanced into the tribes of central Spain, and in the east, to the mouth of the Ebro, and a new base was built at Cartagena, which had obvious advantages over Cadiz as a centre of communications with Carthage. But even in those days, when problems of *Lebensraum* would appear to have involved fewer complications, activities on such a scale could hardly fail to arouse alarm in some quarters: in this case, it was the people of Massilia (Marseilles), of Greek foundation and themselves traders, who felt the need to do something about it.

Appealing to Rome, they succeeded in persuading the Romans in the year 225 B.C. to come to an understanding with Hasdrubal whereby he undertook not to cross to the north bank of the Ebro. Shortly afterward the Romans went one step further; they entered into an alliance with the independent city of Saguntum (the modern Sagunto) 100 miles or so south of the Ebro. The motives for this action are difficult to define. It is possible that the representations of the Massiliots had opened their eyes to a growing peril. But it is difficult to see in Saguntum an effective 'listening' post inside enemy territory; for when war did come the Romans were singularly unprepared for it. It seems more likely that the initiative in the matter of the alliance came from the Saguntines and that the Romans, indifferent to the reactions of the Carthaginians, saw no reason to refuse the request.

However, in 221 B.C. Hasdrubal fell a victim to the sword of a local assassin with a personal grievance, and was succeeded by his brother-in-law, Hannibal, son of

Hamilcar: and within the short space of two years the plans so carefully prepared by Hamilcar Barca with the connivance, if not the enthusiastic support, of the home government in Carthage, were ready to be put into action. The first essential requirement envisaged in the plans had been a standing army of proved worth and reliability, in contrast to the makeshift force of mercenaries which it had usually been the lot of Carthaginian generals to command.

Such an army was now to hand, seasoned by regular campaigning against the native Iberians of central Spain and trained over that exacting terrain to give of their best on the minimum of commissariat. An army that could live on the bare *meseta* of Spain was likely by comparison to find the south of France and Italy lands of milk and honey: and the fact that this army had at its head one of the great generals of history may well have been one of the things that Hamilcar dreamed about—for he was obviously a man who did dream dreams. Did he not take his son Hannibal, as a very small boy, into the temple of Moloch in Carthage before he embarked on his Spanish project and exact from him at the altar an oath that he would ever be an enemy of the Romans?

The first move, therefore, in what came to be known as the Second Punic War was made by Hannibal. In the spring of 219 B.C. he launched an attack on the city of Saguntum, lately allied to the Romans, and after a desperate siege of eight months, captured it. This action left neither the Romans nor the Carthaginians in Carthage in any doubt that they were at war: Hannibal may well have wished to serve notice of his intentions as much upon his own people as upon his enemies.

After wintering at Cartagena, he set out in the spring of 218 B.C. on the great adventure of the overland journey to Italy. Reckless though it was, the stakes were high. Once inside Italy—and with control of the sea in Roman hands he had no alternative to the overland route—he gambled on receiving support from the Gauls in the Po valley, who had recently been subdued by the Romans, and on causing the Roman federation to disintegrate by his very presence with a victorious army, certainly sufficiently to induce the Romans to restore the *status quo* that existed before the First Punic War. It was a gamble that nearly came off. But to say more at the moment would be to anticipate, if not actually digress from the subject of this book.

There are no passages in classical literature that indicate with any precision at all by which route Hannibal and his army left Spain. Livy mentions that it was a pass and that, subsequent to the crossing, encampment was made at the modern town of Elne: this reference would strongly suggest Le Perthus as the place of exit and common sense reinforces it. Hannibal obviously intended to reach Italy before the autumn of the same year and with an army that could average only 7 miles per day, he could afford few deviations from the nearest route. Le Perthus, being only 900 feet high, was likely to provide few obstacles.

Meanwhile, the Romans appear to have been remarkably unaware of what was literally coming to them. The siege of Saguntum had given them a year's warning, but when the campaigning season of 218 B.C. opened, we find but four legions mobilised, only a small fraction of the man-power available. Two separate expeditions were being mounted, one under the consul Sempronius to invade North Africa from Sicily, the other under the command of the other consul, Publius Scipio, to proceed by sea to friendly Marseilles and using that city as a base, to undertake the expulsion of the Carthaginians from Spain.

Startling news, however, greeted the second expeditionary force on its arrival at the mouth of the Rhone. Hannibal and his army were already east of the river, heading for the Alps and Northern Italy. Scipio seems to have been scarcely able to credit this report. He hurriedly sent out a small mounted party to investigate and, when the story was confirmed, he took the decisive step of sending his forces on into Spain under the command of his brother Cnaeus whilst he himself returned by sea alone to Northern Italy to take command of the new forces that his government would now obviously need to put into the field. Thus it was that in the late summer of 218 B.C. two Roman legions landed at Emporiae, just within the borders of Spain. They and their successors were to remain on Spanish soil for more than six hundred years.

CHAPTER II

The Cockpit 218–206 B.C.

IT was obviously sound policy for the Romans to extend their bridgehead and get themselves room for manœuvre as quickly as possible. Accordingly, in September of the same year, Cnaeus Scipio led his forces swiftly south and, surprising the Carthaginians under their commander Hanno at Cissa, a place not now apparently identifiable, a few miles up the river Francoli from Tarragona, won a victory that gave him all Spain north of the Ebro and left him the port of Tarragona itself to serve as his advance supply base.

The counter-stroke was delayed until the early summer of 217 B.C. The chief Carthaginian commander in Spain was Hannibal's own brother Hasdrubal, and it was he who appeared, with superior forces on both land and sea, and encamped at the mouth of the Ebro. The challenge was one that needed to be met at once, for too much was at stake. The Romans could not with equanimity contemplate the possibility of reinforcements in any number being free to join Hannibal in Italy, and the people of Marseilles, now committed to the side of the Romans, were fully aware that they lay directly in the path of any second force on its way to Italy.

It may, therefore, be no mere coincidence that a fragment of the Greek historian, Sosinus, specifically attributes the Roman success that followed to the skill and daring of the Massiliot sailors. Scipio attacked the forty vessels of the enemy with his own thirty-five, and with negligible losses to himself destroyed six and captured twenty-five. Despairing of success in the immediate future, Hasdrubal summarily retired to Cartagena without committing his army, and although Cnaeus Scipio was now rejoined by his brother and senior officer, Publius, who arrived with 8,000 men and twenty more warships, for the rest of this year and for all of the next the Romans did not feel justified in extending their lines of communication to the extent of taking the fight to their enemies, but contented themselves with reconnaissances in force as far south as Saguntum: the Carthaginians for their part had their hands full with a rebellion of the Turdetani in Andalusia.

Beyond all doubt, these two seasons of inactivity were forced upon the Romans in the first place by the drastic events in Italy, where three battles in a row—Trebia, Trasimene and Cannae—had been lost to Hannibal, the last with appalling casualties. Secondly, they were strangers in a strange land, and whilst it would be silly to suggest that the Romans were at any time seriously deterred by the facts of geography, there were in Spain rivers, for instance, larger and more difficult to cross than any in Italy save the Po, with which they had not hitherto been greatly concerned.

Indeed, before the Romans are embarked on major campaigns it would not be inappropriate briefly to set forth the main geographical features of the Peninsula: for, as always, they dictate to some extent, not, perhaps so much how events shall go, but where they will take place.

In general, Spain is corrugated by three parallel mountain ranges that run from east to west, the Cantabrians in the north, the Sierras in the south with the Guadarramas in the centre, with a high plateau, over 2,000 feet above sea-level, linking the central range with the other two. The main rivers, therefore, correspondingly run more or less parallel with the hills, the Ebro from west to east and the Douro, Tagus, Guadiana and Guadalquivir in descending order, from east to west. Apart, therefore, from the coastal fringe, Roman penetration in either a military or economic sense was almost inevitably bound to follow the lines of the valleys, particularly that of the Guadalquivir, which was not only the most fertile, but also the most accessible to the Carthaginians.

But to resume. By the summer of 215 B.C. Hasdrubal felt himself in a position to take the initiative once more. Not only had he received considerable reinforcements from North Africa himself, but a separate army under the command of Himilco came to hold down that part of the south that had recently given trouble. The result of this initiative was the battle of Tortosa, and this second engagement on the Ebro ended no less disastrously for the Carthaginians than the first. The battle, however, was not without its technical interest: both sides were fairly evenly matched, each having some 25,000 men available. It is clear that Hasdrubal was imitating the highly successful tactics of his brother Hannibal, whose method was to give way in the centre and strike the advancing enemy so hard from the wings as to outflank and destroy him. An essential feature of the plan was that the weakened centre should give ground, but not be broken; and it is an interesting side-light on Hannibal's character that in all his battles with the Romans he posted himself in the middle of that all-important centre, because, if the centre were overrun, he did not wish to survive a lost fight. But at Tortosa the centre of the line failed to hold, and Hasdrubal's defeat was complete. As for the Romans, victory established them still more firmly in Spain, and not for the last time in the history of empires a home front was sustained in its darkest hour by the news of stirring deeds on distant shores.

One result of this decisive Roman success was the transfer of allegiance from Carthage to Rome on the part of a large proportion of the Celtiberian tribes of the interior and the consequent loss to the Carthaginians of a fertile ground for the recruitment of new forces: and it was to prevent a further deterioration of the position that the Carthaginian Government diverted to Spain a considerable body of reinforcements that had been intended for Hannibal in Italy. But worse was to follow. For during the next three years (214-212 B.C.) Hasdrubal had to return to North Africa to deal with the defection of a section of the powerful Numidian tribes, leaving the Romans virtually free to do their will in Spain. The two Scipios embarked on a series of victorious offensives that won for them the description of the two thunderbolts of war. Details, however, are not available. Saguntum, Livy tells us, was retaken in 212 B.C.: but that would not, at that date, be spectacular. The historian, Appian, mentions that a section of the Roman army wintered (212-211 B.C.) at Castulo (the modern Cazlona, south-east of Linares), which would indicate a more impressive advance. Certainly by the time that Hasdrubal was free to return in force to Spain in the autumn of 212 B.C. the Romans had divided their strength; Publius Scipio was preparing to winter at Castulo; his brother Cnaeus at Urso (modern Osuna). This division had proved useful in providing a wider range of action against native tribes, but in the following campaigning season it was to prove fatal. Deserted by their Celtiberian mercenaries, both sections suffered disastrous defeat; both Scipios lost their lives, Cnaeus twenty-nine days after his brother, at Lorca. A remnant succeeded in making its way back to the Ebro, and contrived to maintain the allegiance of the tribes north of the river; but to the south, all seemed lost with the possible exception of the fortified towns of Castulo (Cazlona) and Siguenza.

The Romans were thus once more thrust back upon the defensive, and the appointment to the command in Spain of Claudius Nero, a disciple of the Fabian school of warfare, appears to have provided official confirmation of this. But this policy was decisively reversed with the arrival at Emporiae late in the following year (210 B.C.) of Publius Scipio, to take over from Nero. This young man, not more than twenty-five years of age, son of his late father of like name, had received his appointment thanks to a piece of perspicacity rarely shown by a popular assembly. Constitutional precedent had been brushed aside: for normally only men who had been praetors or consuls were eligible for a command in the field. But in this case unorthodoxy was to be amply justified. For, learning that the Carthaginians had concentrated their forces at the mouth of the Tagus, near the Pillars of Hercules, and in the centre of Spain, Scipio decided upon a swift assault upon the main enemy depot at

Cartagena, and in the early spring of 209 B.C. after forced marches from Tarragona, appeared outside the defences of the port and within forty-eight hours had succeeded in capturing it by a series of most resourceful tactics, the final denouement of which was the surprising of the defenders from the rear, by picked troops wading across the lagoon. The prize so swiftly gained was a rich one: enormous quantities of military stores and treasure, and not least in importance, many hostages guaranteeing the good conduct of the Celtiberians of the interior. Among the latter was a young girl of exceptional beauty, as several ancient historians almost seem to delight in recording. Although brought to the notice of the Roman commander, she was sent back unharmed to her betrothed, a young native chieftain. This incident is not out of keeping with what we know otherwise of Scipio's character. He was, for instance, something of a mystic, indulging in long vigils of prayer. But, on a lower estimate, the story may well have been invented by later Roman historians as evidence of 'correctness' on the part of the conquerors.

It may well be that Scipio's dashing exploit in seizing Cartagena was no more than a desperate attempt to stop the Carthaginians by a powerful counterstroke from despatching a relief force to Hannibal in Italy, while the Romans in Spain were temporarily incapacitated. If this was so, then the plan failed, for early in the campaigning season of the following year (208 B.C.) Scipio again advanced from Tarragona and, finding Hasdrubal ensconced in a very strong position of his own choosing at Bailen, made a direct assault upon him, with the result that Hasdrubal had to pull out to the north to avoid serious loss. Pausing on the Tagus only long enough to receive new drafts, with an army now estimated to be 20,000 strong, Hasdrubal passed safely out of Spain by the Atlantic seaboard and made tracks for Italy. Scipio has been criticised by both ancient and modern writers for his failure to prevent the departure of these reinforcements for Hannibal. But such criticism ignores difficulties of supply with which the Romans in Spain were always beset. One army might pursue another along the valley of a Spanish river and hope still to find sufficient supplies on which to keep going: to pursue an enemy who was still in good order over the high plateau of the interior was to invite disaster by famine.

But Carthage had already paid a heavy price for the despatch of these troops: in the following year, 207 B.C., she was to pay more. With Hasdrubal gone, Mago, now senior Carthaginian commander in Spain, joined forces with the third army, which all this time had been based on Cadiz, and was brought to battle by Scipio in this year at Ilipa (probably identifiable as Alcala del Rio, near Seville). There he suffered a decisive defeat. Polybius has left a long but somewhat confused account of the battle. Scipio seems, for once, to have adopted Hannibal's tactics of inviting attack in the centre, but how the Carthaginian superiority in cavalry was discounted is never made clear. But there is no doubt that after this battle there was no effective fighting force left to oppose the Romans and the last year of the war in Spain (206 B.C.), apart from some trouble with tribes north of the Ebro, was devoted to the mopping up of isolated pockets of resistance based on such towns as Lorca and Castax and, further west, Astapa (modern Estepa in Andalusia, between Osuna and Puente Genil) and Cadiz: actually the last-named town surrendered of its own free will when Mago, who had survived the battle of Ilipa, left it to make a desperate and unavailing assault upon Cartagena. Repelled from there, he sailed away to the Balearic Islands, where Mahon, the capital of Minorca, bears his name. Cadiz, as a reward, received the status of a free city. Scipio founded the first Roman colony in Spain at Italica (Santiponce, north-west of Seville) and, his task now completed, left for Rome to stand for the consulship of 205 B.C.

CHAPTER III

The Unavailing Struggle 206–133 B.C.

DURING the twelve years now ended by the departure of Scipio from their shores, the policy of the native Iberians had not unnaturally been one of vacillation: and it is not one that necessarily incurs discredit for its makers. It is true that Livy, in his account of these years, often mentions the untrustworthiness of native mercenaries, but as such remarks are almost invariably a prelude to the admission of a Roman reverse, the reliability of the remarks themselves may well be open to question. But it is likely that the Iberians as a whole had little love for either the Carthaginians or the Romans. Never, of course, a single political entity, but, by the endless number of their small communities, showing a distinct inclination towards anarchy, in the course of the three hundred years that the Carthaginians were in Spain they had, in part, come to terms with them in the fertile valleys of the south and the adjacent mining districts, but the majority had been left alone: for the primary interest of the invaders had been trade not empire.

But now the Carthaginians were gone and in their place stood the Romans. They, too, were interested in commerce and trade, but in addition it was a national characteristic of theirs never to leave a job half-finished with untidy ends. They were later, for instance, to be dissatisfied with the untidy edge that Hadrian's Wall represented for them in Britain. The Elbe would always have been, in their opinion, a neater boundary than the Rhine. So in their first major conquest beyond the borders of Italy, they were never likely to be satisfied with conquest of a vague section of the east and south coast.

Even these restricted conquests were speedily subject to organisation. Two provinces were created, Hither and Further Spain, separated by the little river of Almanzora, near the township of Beria (Vera, about halfway between modern Cartagena and Almeria). Hither Spain did not extend deep from the east coast except up the Ebro valley, where it reached modern Saragossa and Huesca: the northern boundary of Further Spain was represented roughly by the Sierra Morena.

Both provinces were rich prizes economically: there were extensive silver mines near Cartagena where, Polybius tells us, 40,000 slaves were engaged in the second century B.C. Further west, copper had been worked from time immemorial at Luxia (Rio Tinto), there were silver and gold mines in the Sierra Morena, while the valley of the Baetis (Guadalquivir) was rich in wheat, olives and wine. Little that is certain is known of Roman economics at any stage of their history: they were obviously by the nature of things less complicated than those of our own times. But when we read that between the years 206-197 B.C. 130,000 lb. of silver and 4,000 lb. of gold were shipped to Rome, it is clear that these commodities were highly valued then as they would be now; indeed, for a parallel influx of similar metals, one's mind goes forward seventeen hundred years to the time when Spain herself was the recipient of the treasures of Mexico and Peru.

Such Iberian communities as had been in the power of the Carthaginians now had the Romans for masters, but the terms of their subjection are nowhere clearly defined: they do not appear, however, to have paid a corn tithe as did Sicily at this time, but rather a fixed sum (stipendium) payable in gold and silver, partly in the form of bullion, partly in coinage: for the mintage of Iberian money started soon after the Roman occupation began, coins of this era having been found as belonging to the towns of Emporiae, Lerida and Sagunto: while Huesca seems to have been an important mint.

But still harder for the local population to bear were the private depredations that the governor of the province generally saw fit to indulge in: provincial governors were in office as early as 205 B.C. After 197 B.C. appointments were normally reserved for men who had served as praetors in Rome, and although for one year only, they were often extended for a second year: in fact, these depredations assumed such scandalous proportions that in the year 171 B.C. there was established in Rome a court of enquiry into such activities, where it was hoped that the victims might secure redress. But the hope was, in the main, illusory: the ignorance, illiteracy and remoteness of the plaintiffs were serious handicaps and juries too often were drawn from among those very people who either had profited in this way in the past or had hopes of so doing in the future. Almost exactly one hundred years later, it was an act of great political courage for Cicero to prosecute Verres on behalf of the Sicilians, and signal proof of his forensic genius that he should succeed.

Small surprise, therefore, that these grievances, coupled with the liability, common to all subject peoples, to provide auxiliary troops in considerable numbers, led to an insurrection in the year 197 B.C. that spread rapidly over half the area of Spain. It is significant that the trouble started with the unwarlike Turdetani in the Ronda-Huelva area and with the peaceable trading towns of Malnaga ad Sexi (Almunecar, to the east of Malaga). Before the close of the year the Nearer Province was involved: for here, we read, the praetor in charge suffered defeat at the hands of local forces. In the following year a Roman victory was recorded at Turta, an unidentified place in the Turdetani country, but the effects of it can only have been temporary, for in the year 195 B.C. there arrived in Emporiae from Italy two full legions under the command of the consul Marcus Cato the Elder, destined later as soldier, author and statesman to be one of the most imposing figures in Roman political life of the second century B.C. He, or his army, proved impressive enough even at this stage of his career. Making a reconnaissance in force, he moved down Spain, bringing at least a momentary peace wherever he went, succouring the governor of the Further Province in particular, but without being able to indulge in a single decisive action, the rebels wisely deciding that it took two to start a fight. Indeed, on his way north he made half-hearted attempts to reduce the towns of Siguenza and Numantia and only succeeded in stirring up into active hostility the Celtiberians who lived in those parts, the best fighting men in Spain. But later in the same season he made amends: for by a swift campaign against tribes in the Catalonian hills he brought yet more silver mines into the orbit of Rome.

But the war dragged on: the Lusitanians (of modern Portugal) joined the rebels the next year (194 B.C.) and in subsequent campaigns the Romans from the south reached Toledo, subduing the local tribe, the Oretani. But honours were no more than even when in 190 B.C. Aemilius Paullus, later the conqueror of Macedonia, lost one battle and won one, in an assault upon the Lusitani. If during the next nine years there seem to have been no major developments of any sort until in 181 B.C. the Romans began to penetrate south down the tributaries of the Ebro, it must be remembered that during all these years they were heavily committed to victorious campaigns in Greece and Asia Minor and were thus content with holding actions in Spain. In fact, it was in pursuance of this policy that peace was restored to the country by conciliatory treaties offered to the Celtiberi in particular by the liberal-minded commander of the day, Gracchus, father of the would-be reformers in Rome of 133 B.C. and 123 B.C. Two further Roman towns were founded, Graccuris, near Alfaro, to the south of Calahorra on the Ebro, and Cordoba, and it was clear that more could be gained by clemency than by force of arms.

Historians have little to tell us of the next twenty-five years, and it is tempting to think that subsequent Roman commanders followed where Gracchus had shown the way. The fact that the city of Carteia (on the coast west of Algeciras) was selected, in 171 B.C., as a settlement for the illegitimate children of Roman soldiers would not appear to commit the Romans either way in this respect. But certain it is that in 154 B.C. full-scale rebellion broke out once more. The trouble-makers were again the Lusitani of the far west and the Celtiberi in the centre of the Peninsula. The former were in the field uninterruptedly from 154 B.C. to 138 B.C., the latter from 153 B.C. to 152 B.C. and again from 143 B.C. to 133 B.C. The Lusitani won early successes. Invading the Further Province, they brought the Roman governor to an action and inflicted casualties estimated at 9,000, and captured standards were sent to rouse the Celtiberi to revolt.

The gesture was well-timed. That section of the Celtiberi who lived nearest to the Hither Province had become involved in hostilities with the Romans by building a tribal fortress for themselves at Segeda (near Belmonte del Peregil, 12 kms. south-east of Calatayud on the Madrid-Saragossa road). The Romans, temporarily free to give their full attention to Spain, did not underestimate the gravity of the position. From this date until the end of the war in 133 B.C. they superseded the praetors who, after their year of office in Rome, had passed to the governorship of a Spanish province, and automatically to the command of the troops in the province, by the appointment of consuls, in like manner, at the end of their year of office: they even altered the date of the beginning of the official year from March 1st to January 1st, so that the new consul could be at the head of his troops in distant Spain in good time for the start of the campaigning season.

So it was Nobilior, the consul of 153 B.C., who, surviving a defeat near Almazan on August 23rd in his advance upon the native strongpoint of Numantia (8 kms. north of Soria), was still able to encamp on the hill Gran Atalaya, four miles east of that town, a site that is identifiable to this day. From this base, he made unavailing assaults upon both Numantia and

Uxama (Osma) before the Castilian winter confined him to his quarters. Nobilior's successor in the following year preferred to negotiate peace and, despite great provocation from the Roman commander in 151 B.C. —who treacherously seized Cauca (modern Coca, near Segovia) and made abortive attempts to take Intercatia (50 kms. north of Zamora) and Pallentia (Palencia)—peace of a kind did prevail and the Lusitani were left to carry on alone. Their first reaction was to accept the peace terms offered by the Roman M. Atilius, but in 151 B.C. they were up in arms against his successor Galba and inflicted a sharp defeat on him near Carmo (Carmona). Galba's answer was to indulge in a piece of flagrant bad faith. Assembling a large section of the fighting forces of the Lusitani under pretence of making them an offer of land, he treacherously put them to the sword and few escaped. Roman historians have not cared to identify for us the scene of this outrage, but on his return to Rome as a private citizen, Galba was impeached by the veteran Cato, anxious for the good name of his country.

For a few years, however, this act of treachery served the Romans well; for the Lusitani were temporarily crippled. But vengeance was not long delayed. By 147 B.C. a fighting force of some 10,000 men was available under the command of the youthful Viriathus, who had been one of the few survivors of the massacre four years before and was thus left with a special legacy of hatred for the Romans. His first success came in the same year; some 4,000 Romans were ambushed in the Sierra Ronda and put to the sword. Emboldened by this success, Viriathus advanced during the next campaigning season into the La Mancha territory, centre of the Carpetani tribe, claimed another 4,000 victims in defeating the praetor Plautius, and, establishing himself in the fastness of the 'Hill of Venus' (Sierra San Vincente), terrorised the whole of the surrounding countryside, advancing, on one occasion, over the Guadarramas to Segovia. This state of affairs he was able to maintain over the next three years, the position not being materially affected even by the arrival of a consular army of two legions.

When, therefore, in the year 143 B.C. the Celtiberi were prevailed upon to renew the hostilities they had so tamely dropped eight years before, Viriathus began to seem capable of achieving a permanent solution. But in the end the inability of the Iberians effectively to unite proved fatal for his plans. But he came very near to succeeding; in 141 B.C. another consular army was so thoroughly harassed that, when eventually surrounded, it surrendered.

It was now that Viriathus faltered: possibly because he sensed that his followers were beginning to weary of the long war, he allowed his defenceless enemy to depart in exchange for a treaty of doubtful value. The Romans had the grace to accept the treaty and they stood by it for one year, but their commander of the following year, one Servilius Caepio, had little compunction in renewing the fight and even less in making up for his lack of success in the field by bribing three of Viriathus's friends to murder him. This was in the year 138 B.C., and with his death the Lusitanian war collapsed. Never again were the Iberians to have so great a leader of their own. Almost always victorious, he had fallen in the end only to an assassin's sword. With his death, modern Portugal passed into the hands of Rome, but only as a kind of annexe to the Further

Province: the establishment of a third province of Lusitania was still a long way off.

In the meantime the war against the Celtiberi seems to have been conducted as a separate campaign under an entirely different set of commanders and in the main, for the whole of its length (143-133 B.C.), it revolved upon the siege of Numantia. Metellus in the first two years crushed all native opposition in the Jalon river basin, south of the Ebro, but had to leave the assault upon Numantia to his successor, Pompeius, who, in two years, proved incapable of taking the town either by direct assault or by siege, although his forces outnumbered the 8,000 defenders by nearly four to one: his main camp is still visible on the hill of Castillejo. In the end Pompeius negotiated a peace and the Numantians handed over thirty pieces of silver which were not returned when, characteristically—for this was the third time in twelve years that bad faith had been shown—the Roman Senate refused to ratify the arrangement.

Thereafter, under Pompeius' successor (139-138 B.C.) the morale of the Roman forces investing Numantia was in marked decline and matters reached a head under Mancinus (in 137 B.C.) who, after a series of reverses, turned and fled towards the Ebro, only to capitulate, with 20,000 men, to opponents with less than one-third of that total. Again by a combination of magnanimity on the one side and of double-dealing on the other, the Romans escaped with their lives. But the generals who followed Mancinus did not dare to renew the direct assault on Numantia, and it was largely a position of stalemate that greeted the arrival in Spain in 134 B.C. of Scipio Aemilianus, son of the conqueror of Macedon, adopted into the famous family of the Scipios, and now summoned by popular clamour

Tarragona. The Aqueduct

Above. Tarragona. Tower of the Scipios

Right. Aqueduct at Segovia

to take command in Spain on the strength of his destruction of Carthage twelve years before.

From the start Scipio decided to take Numantia by siege rather than by assault, a decision probably influenced by the calibre of the troops at his disposal: so, after some weeks of practice at entrenchment, he began to advance up the Ebro in the late summer of the same year, just in time to forestall the Numantians in the replenishment of their grain stores from the harvest. Arriving outside Numantia by about October, he immediately set about the complete circumvallation of the town with a full circle of walls and intermittent towers. To house the 60,000 men under his command, seven camps were constructed, the sites of all of which have been revealed by excavation. Scipio's own camp was on the hill of Castillejo, half a mile to the north of the town, the same site used by Pompeius six years before. Scipio's brother commanded the camp to the south of the town at Peña Rodonda. These two camps contained the legionary forces, the other five the Italian and Iberian auxiliaries, who amounted to about two-thirds of the total forces engaged. The inevitable end came during the next year, 133 B.C.: the Numantians had made an ineffectual attempt to get honourable terms and had even had recourse to cannibalism before surrendering, and many of the 4,000 defenders slew themselves rather than live to grace a conqueror's triumph.

Without waiting for senatorial permission, Scipio razed Numantia to the ground and, as he had had previous practice at Carthage, he made a good job of it. Numantia never again emerged as a living community and with its fall the first phase of Spain's long struggle for freedom was over.

CHAPTER IV

Spain under the Republic

WITH this decisive defeat of her efforts to throw off the Roman yoke, Spain passed into a condition of anonymity: war being 'news' to ancient historians as it is still to journalists of today, she was left to make what she could of the 'pax Romana' in almost complete obscurity, once the fighting and the shouting had died down. But from what is known from other sources of the organisation of provincial government under the Republic, it is possible to make some assessment of conditions in Spain during these unchronicled years.

In the first place, although the Romans now had more or less effective control of a much larger area of Spain—viz. all land east of modern Portugal as far north as the Douro and south of a line from the Douro to Bilbao—the two-province system was still maintained under the same names. Whereas some seventy years before at the end of their initial successes, when Spain represented only their second province, they had shown some alacrity and drive in organising the newly acquired territory, it was an entirely different story now: with Greece, some parts of Asia Minor and a section of North Africa to cope with in addition, no wonder the archaic machinery of government was beginning to creak: a city council was proving but a poor instrument for the government of an empire.

Perhaps the most obvious deficiency was on the military side: the Roman army traditionally was a citizen militia, under the command of amateurs as represented by the elected consuls of the year, the twin heads of state: and although a citizen army had, in the end, emerged with credit from the war with Hannibal and later proved good enough to win the decisive battles that brought the expansion towards the east, there had been plenty of instances in Spain alone of crude amateurism at the top involving Roman arms in needless disaster. Nowhere was the professionalism of a standing army missed more than in the garrisoning of the provinces. Since the citizen-soldier was regarded as a fighting man only for an emergency, there were few troops available to be placed by the senate at the disposal of a new governor. And what of the subject peoples, the provincials themselves? In war, they might serve as auxiliaries to the Roman legions proper: in peace they were disarmed, unless, having specialist qualifications as cavalrymen, slinger or engineer, individuals found more permanent employment.

There was weakness in provincial administration as well: and this, too, began at the top, where the system of election to a provincial governorship was haphazard in the extreme. Men who had served their year in Rome as consul or praetor could expect in the following year to proceed to the governorship of a province of one year's duration, but the second post often called for far different qualities from those exercised in the first. A man was, in any case, often elevated to consulship or praetorship for quite unworthy reasons connected with local politics: and even where the candidates were sound, it was a drawing of lots that decided which province each should take. Common sense did, however, prevail in some respects: it was a poor governor indeed who did not have his year of office expanded to two and, in an emergency, popular opinion could secure the appointment to a province of a suitable person who had not previously held magisterial office: the two Scipios of 210 B.C. and 134 B.C. were notable examples. A further fault was the complete absence of any kind of permanent Civil Service in the province: each governor arrived—and departed—with his long retinue of minor officers and prefects (to whom he could delegate responsibility) and a whole host of secretaries, attendants, doctors, soothsayers and town-criers, most, if not all, of whom would be glad to feather their nests during their short stay. That the judiciary should rest in the hands of the Roman governor, assisted by a body of Romans resident in the province, would appear to complete a vicious ring of exploitation; on the other hand, as between Spaniard and Spaniard, it probably meant that some measure of impartial judgement was available where none had been before.

It was not until the dictatorship of Caesar, at the very end of the Republican period, that any serious attempt was made to extend the Roman franchise to the provinces: indeed, up to that time there had been active prejudice against any such move. It took four years of Social War before full citizenship was conferred in 88 B.C. on all Italians living south of the Po. There was particularly strong resentment against granting it to whole provincial communities, such as cities. Italica and Cordoba were two such favoured cities in Spain, but the former owed its foundation to the popular general Scipio in 206 B.C., the latter to a temporary policy of comparative appeasement in 179 B.C. On the other hand, it was quite commonly awarded to individuals and, in the course of the Social War mentioned above, a whole squadron of Spanish cavalry received the award. But, in any event, compared with the eastern provinces, which were well stocked with cities of Greek foundation, Spain had very few cities and the policy of urbanisation was not noticeably developed there until the early days of the Empire.

Taxation in Spain during this period is likely to have taken the form of a fixed sum, a 'stipendium' agreed upon after negotiations between the Roman authorities and the many tribal communities: and even if 'publicani' (the publicans of the New Testament) were not needed for the collection of these, they would certainly be needed to deal with the yield of harbour taxes and of the mines which were all, at this time, private enterprises.

Not all the wealth thus collected was lost to the country: some of it was obviously used on development schemes. Naturally, not much building still standing can specifically be said to belong to this period: but certainly by the year 120 B.C. the Via Maxima from Le Perthus to Cadiz via the east and south coast was in existence, complete with milestones, if we may believe Polybius. The Porta Popilia at Cartagena may well date from the year 139 B.C., named after a consul of that year, while much of the lower levels of the massive walls at Saguntum probably date from Republican times: and if all this seems but poor comfort for the Spaniards if, in fact, all the deficiencies that have been mentioned, add up in the opinions of some to a general indictment of Rome and the Romans, let it be borne in mind that by the standards of their own pre-Christian day, they were not unmerciful: let it rather be laid to their credit that in such things as the institution of a court of redress for provincials there can be recognised the beginnings of an organised public conscience.

In the meantime there were isolated incidents that caught the attention of contemporary historians. In 123 B.C. one of the consuls of that year undertook the annexation of the Balearic Islands, from which pirates, who infested the whole of the Mediterranean in varying degrees, had presumably been interfering with the Roman sea-route to Spain. Special protection, we are told, was improvised on board the invading ships against the slingers for which the islands were famous. Two colonies were founded at Palma and Pollentia, Roman citizens resident in Spain being, rather oddly, withdrawn to form the necessary nucleus of population.

The second incident well illustrates the weakness of provincial defences under the Republic: in the last decade of the second century B.C. there occurred one of those periodic invasions of nomadic tribes which had, on occasion, particularly in 390 B.C., shaken Rome to the core. This time the invaders were the Cimbri and Teutones of Germanic stock. On October 6th, 105 B.C., finding two Roman armies near Orange in Provence under the divided leadership of the two consuls of the year, they engaged each in quick succession and inflicted upon them a joint total of 80,000 casualties. The Cimbri were now free in the following year to enter Spain, which they did via Puigcerda; but, harassed by the local Celtiberi and disheartened by the rigours of the Aragonese plateau, they retired again beyond the Pyrenees to meet with decisive defeat at the hands of the Roman Marius at Vercellae on the Raudine plain.

But their entrance into Spain appears to have touched off a fresh series of revolts. In fact, the Lusitani must have been in action before this: for we are told that one of the consuls who fell at Orange had previously been accorded a triumph in Rome for his successes against them in the year 107 B.C. Triumphs, however, over unfortunate Spaniards became quite commonplace in the next few years. The fact that the first in 98 B.C. was immediately followed by renewed rebellion is significant. Military command was beginning to be regarded as the highway to success in politics and undoubtedly an element of political propaganda was entering into the granting of them.

But there is no doubt that Titus Didius earned his triumph over the Celtiberi in 93 B.C.: rebellious towns were razed to the ground and Termantia (now Santa Maria de Tiermes, south of the Douro), second only in the old days to Numantia as a defence position, was permanently cleared of its inhabitants. These drastic measures culminated in a treacherous massacre of the Celtiberi under circumstances that recall a similar outrage committed upon the Lusitani by the infamous Galba many years before. Of the merits of a triumph over the Lusitani, granted in this same year also to Didius's colleague, we have no evidence on which to form a judgement, save that the consul of this year of double triumphs was himself called upon during his governorship of the following year to deal out further chastisement.

One of the officers in Didius's forces in action against the Celtiberi had been a certain Quintus Sertorius, destined in the next decade to prove himself, perhaps, the greatest name in Spanish history under Republican Rome. He was an Italian, born in 123 B.C. in the Sabine country near Rome: before his above-mentioned service in Spain he had served with some distinction against the Cimbri and Teutones, surviving the disaster at Arausio and later taking part in the victories of Marius. However, when he offered himself in 88 B.C. as a candidate for a minor political office in Rome, he received a rebuff at the hands of the senatorial party, led by Sulla. By way of clarification it should be stated that in the eighties of this century the latent rivalry between the oligarchical senate and the popular assembly of the people flared up into open violence under their respective military champions, Sulla and Marius. Sertorius, therefore, as a representative of the newly enfranchised Italians, was not acceptable to the conservative Sulla and his consequent rejection at the polls served to identify him with the Marian or popular party, to which he had no genuine attachment. However, it is clear that at some time during the brief period of Marian ascendancy, he served a year as praetor and, when civil war was renewed with Sulla's return from the Mithridatic war in 83 B.C., he was an obvious choice for his party to send to hold Spain for his side.

Arriving in Spain via the Col de Perthus, he took control of the two provinces and spent the following year in organising opposition to Sulla, who was rapidly establishing himself as master of Italy. Early in 81 B.C. the inevitable legions of Sulla—two of them—arrived, and Sertorius, his forces hopelessly outnumbered, fled to North Africa. Here his biographer,

Plutarch, involved him in many hardships and romantic adventures, including an abortive attempt to find peace for his soul on the Isles of the Blessed as represented by Madeira.

Be that as it may, he landed at Belo, just west of Tarifa, one year later, to take command of yet another revolt on the part of the Lusitanians and before the end of the campaigning season, had defeated the governor of Further Spain in an action near the Guadalquivir river and, with 8,000 native troops at his disposal, was in control of the province. The next year brought stiffer fighting, but still more definite success: evading an attempt by the two new provincial governors to trap him between them, he divided his forces, and one section under Lucius Hirtuleius defeated and slew the governor of Hither Spain at Consuegra between the Tagus and the Guadiana and proceeded to overrun that province, whilst Sertorius kept the more formidable Metellus occupied in the south-west.

For more than a year Metellus ranged far and wide—from the Guadarramas to the mouth of the Tagus—in his attempts to crush his elusive enemy, so well-versed in guerrilla tactics. In the end, after being enticed into wasting his substance by undertaking the siege of Lacobriga (now Lagos in the extreme south-west of Portugal) in the remotest depths of a hostile countryside, he was constrained to retire south of the Guadalquivir and leave Sertorius free to extend his control over the whole of Spain between the Sierra Morena and the Pyrenees, and to embark upon the organisation of this territory.

He selected Huesca as his capital and started a school there to which native leaders sent their sons, an arrangement that had presumably political as well as academic advantages. From among his Roman following he appointed an advisory council, 300 strong, and started the development of Denia (north of Alicante) as a naval base for his allies, the pirates, who, for generations, had infested the Mediterranean and ten years later were to provoke the Romans into taking effective action to suppress them. So strong indeed was his position by the end of this year that he was the obvious magnet for dissident Romans, and 20,000 infantry and 1,500 cavalry, representing the remnants of opposition to the Sullan régime in Italy, arrived in Spain from Sardinia under the command of Marcus Perperna.

Meanwhile in Rome itself the Senate, fully alive to the dangers inherent in the Spanish situation, despatched the young Pompey, pupil of Sulla, who still lacked the necessary political qualifications for the post, to restore the position. With his arrival early in the season of 76 B.C. the second phase in the Sertorian war began.

Pompey's first objective was to gain possession of the eastern coastline by simultaneous attack by himself from across the Ebro and from the south by his subordinate, Memmius, who was to be put ashore at Cartagena: Pompey succeeded in forcing the Ebro in spite of opposition from Perperna, but failed, with heavy losses, to relieve the town of Lauro (now an uninhabited site near Puig, between Valentia and Sagunto), which had never accepted Sertorius and was now under siege by him; and he retired tamely once more behind the Ebro. In the meantime, however, Hirtuleius, Sertorius's other lieutenant, was only partially successful in holding Metellus, who, after his losses in the south of Portugal, had not ventured far from his headquarters at Cordoba. Now, emboldened by news of Pompey from the north, he renewed the fight and, astutely enticing Hirtuleius to keep his men standing to for some hours under the hot Andalusian sun of an August day, he routed him in an engagement at Italica and, thus released from his shadow, hurriedly betook himself north, there to join forces with Pompey. The year closed with Pompey engaged on some 'face-saving' operations against Celtiberian communities in the upper Ebro valley, whilst Sertorius, if in need of a lift in morale, received it in the form of an understanding that he reached with Mithridates, Rome's enemy in Asia Minor. Sertorius was fast becoming a figure of international significance.

The campaigning season of 75 B.C. opened with a two-pronged offensive by the government forces. Metellus advanced as far south as Segovia and there defeated Hirtuleius, who was numbered among the slain. Perperna, Sertorius's other lieutenant, was hardly any more successful in dealing with Pompey's thrust down the east coast. He was unable to stop Pompey from entering Valentia, but when the latter, in return, sought to attack the combined forces of Perperna and Sertorius in the nearby valley of the Sucro, he was skilfully outmanœuvred and only rescued by the timely arrival of Metellus from the interior. 'If that old woman had not come up,' Sertorius is quoted as saying, 'I would have thrashed the youngster and sent him back to Rome.'

The result for the rest of the year was an uneasy stalemate. The rebels were shaken by the death of Hirtuleius and retired into Saguntum: Metellus retired into Gaul, whilst Pompey renewed his late-season activities at the top of the Ebro watershed, attacking in particular the town of Clunia and always hoping to draw Sertorius into an action of his own choosing. The winter he spent in Pamplona at the western end of the Pyrenees awaiting the arrival, via Roncesvalles, of the two legions which he had so earnestly requested of the Senate.

These additional legions proved decisive; changing his objective, Pompey attacked the centres of Celtiberian population throughout 74 B.C. He captured Bilbilis (Calatayud) and Segobriga (near Saelices in the district of Cuenca), but Sertorius was able to prevent the fall of Pallentia (Palencia), and before the end of the year inflicted losses amounting to 3,000 in all on the combined forces of Pompey and Metellus at Calagurris (modern Calahorra, north-west of Saragossa); but this was to be his last major success.

The next year brought a rapid deterioration in his position as his support from the natives melted away, a process which his own embitterment did much to accelerate. In the end, a sad and disillusioned man, he fell an almost willing victim to the assassin's hand, that of his lieutenant, Perperna, in 72 B.C. As he left Spain in the following year, Pompey erected a trophy on the summit of the Col de Perthus whereon he claims to have captured over eight hundred 'towns': no mention is made of his valiant opponent.

Scant justice is done to the personality of Sertorius by the prosaic recital of recorded facts: although in the end he must be classified as a failure, it is evident that there were in him strong elements of greatness. The German historian Mommsen would have him recognised as possibly the greatest man that Rome had hitherto produced: and it is indeed tempting to suggest that, aware of the grave constitutional weaknesses in a city-state controlling a world-wide empire, he intended to apply those remedial measures that Caesar was to employ some thirty years later. But a sober estimate of the man is sufficient to warrant our attention without indulging in mere speculation. As a soldier, he combined sound experience with rare gifts of leadership and a power for swift and daring movements that often left his enemies bewildered. He found excellent material in the Spanish hillmen and made them the equals of the redoubtable Roman legions. His understanding of (and possibly his affection for) the Spanish people made them willing tools in his hands. He was aware of their delight in bright colours and introduced them into both their weapons and their clothing. He had the necessary degree of showmanship; a white fawn perpetually attended him, and as it was a symbol of his communion with the gods, there was great consternation when it was temporarily lost in the battle on the Sucro river in 75 B.C. That he was a romantic, not without vision, is suggested by his contemplation of a life in the Isles of the Blessed; nor did he lack the requisite ruthlessness, though in his last two years it may well have been ruthlessness born of despair. That he negotiated a limited agreement with Mithridates, the enemy of his country, can be taken as the measure of his hatred for the Sullan régime in Rome: that he failed in the end may have been inevitable, though there is no greater pitfall for the student of history than to think that, because an event did happen, it was bound to happen. It would be more perspicacious to say that he failed to forge a strong enough army as a weapon for his hand. Two decades later Julius Caesar did not make the same mistake.

CHAPTER V

Spain and Julius Caesar

THE name of Caesar pervaded the whole Roman world in the middle of the last century before Christ, but it is associated with Spain as much as with any other part of the Empire and more than with most. Born in 100 B.C. into one of the oldest aristocratic families in Rome, possibly through his connection by marriage with the great proletarian Marius he had developed—or been credited with—sympathies with the popular party. His early years lacked distinction: he was much more the young aristocrat enjoying himself than the earnest budding soldier or politician with a plan to save the world. Nothing is more remarkable in Caesar's whole career than the late hour at which he started it.

Indeed, some remorse for opportunities lost in youth came to him when he visited the famous sanctuary of Hercules on the island of Sanctipetri (18 kms. south of Cadiz). There, confronted by the statue of Alexander the Great, appropriately enough, in the temple of a god so beloved of soldiers, he lamented the fact that, whereas he himself had achieved nothing, Alexander had, at that age, already conquered the world. This was in the year 68 B.C. when he was elected to quaestorship, the first rung of the political ladder that led to the consulship, and was appointed to the staff of the governor of Further Spain of that year.

It could be argued that this was the year of his regeneration, if ever there was any such; for both his later biographers, Suetonius and Plutarch, proceed to relate the story of a dream he dreamt, in which he offered violence to his own mother: when the mother is interpreted as Mother Earth, it is obvious that he is destined for a great future. Suetonius describes this dream as occurring on the night of the visit to the temple of Hercules. Now the whole story may well be a piece of embroidery, devised later to fit the subject. But it is an interesting point that at this time on the little island of San Sebastian, west of Cadiz, there was an oracular temple of Venus, which operated through the interpretation of the dreams of the visitors who stayed there.

Caesar proceeded to a praetorship in Rome in 62 B.C., and in the following year came back to Further Spain as its governor, returning to Rome in time to secure the consulship for the year 59 B.C. He left behind him in Rome many personal debts, and it may have been with something of a fellow feeling that he effected a satisfactory settlement of war debts involving the province. At least one historian, unsympathetic to Caesar, declares that he lost no opportunity of acquiring the means to settle his own debts. But in any event such action was neither unprecedented nor, in his case, significant: what was significant was his first experience of the art of military command. No other of the world's great generals was so late in entering upon the career that brought him fame.

With no more likely motive than personal ambition, he started a campaign to subdue that section of modern

Portugal between the Tagus and the Douro, and was involved in some hard fighting in the Sierra de Estrella, the defenders of which retreated to the island of Peniche (45 kms. north of Lisbon). Later in the campaign, by combined operations on land and sea, he invaded Galicia and reached and captured Brigantium (Coruña), thus completing the subjection of the west coast of the Peninsula: so at one and the same time he won himself a triumph in Rome and discovered his latent abilities as a soldier.

Many fateful events were to be enacted before he returned eleven years later. He entered the first Triumvirate with Pompey and Crassus—the latter a representative of business interests—to rig the politics of what proved to be the last years of the Republic. After his consulship in 59 B.C. he proceeded to the conquest of Gaul, and at the Conference of Lucca in Northern Italy in 56 B.C., new life was put into the waning Triumvirate: Caesar's command in Gaul was extended. Pompey and Crassus became consuls for the year 55 B.C. and thereafter Spain and Syria were to become their respective provinces for extended periods.

Pompey never arrived in his, but stayed somewhat ill at ease in Rome, contenting himself with sending reliable deputies, in the persons of Afranius and Petreius, to take charge of the two Spanish provinces: Crassus hurried off to his province and, as it proved, to his death, at the misguided battle of Carrhae in the following year. His passing served but to render more obvious the rift between Caesar and Pompey, a rift that was inevitable in any event, if we credit the former with having laid his plans many years in advance. On January 11th in the year 49 B.C. Caesar crossed the Rubicon (the little river that divided his province from

Theatre at Saguntum

Section of the ruins of Numantia

Arch at Medinaceli

Italy proper) and the civil war was begun. Within a few short weeks Pompey had evacuated his troops from Brindisi to Greece, leaving Italy to its fate. So the first round went to Caesar. The second was to be fought in Spain; for Caesar had little choice in the matter: not possessing any fleet, he was incapable of pursuing Pompey himself. But no fleet was necessary for reaching Spain, which he knew to be strongly held for Pompey by seven legions under Afranius and Petreius.

Under his instructions, therefore, early in the spring of 49 B.C., his lieutenant Fabius moved, via Puigcerda, into Spain with the three legions he had in Gaul and proceeded down the Segre valley to Ilerda (Lerida), where he found Afranius and Petreius with five of their seven legions strongly entrenched on the heights of Gardeny, barely half a mile to the south-west of the town, which was itself strongly garrisoned and commanded the one stone bridge over the river. There, a little to the north of the town, Fabius made his camp and settled down to wait for Caesar. But the situation was not an easy one: the enemy had seen to it that no supplies were available any longer on the north side of the river, and two new bridges, 4 miles apart, had to be improvised by the Caesarians above the town to facilitate the fetching of them. Even so, a sudden spring flood destroyed the lower one (at Corbins) and Fabius had to move smartly over the other (at Termens) to rescue one of his legions, engaged in foraging, from the clutches of Afranius, who had speedily seen his opportunity.

Caesar arrived with three more legions on May 2nd and in accordance with his need for a speedy and, if possible, inexpensive victory lost no time in offering battle to the Pompeian leaders ensconced on Gardeny. They refused it, as it was their policy to keep Caesar engaged on a long and indecisive campaign while the Senate and Pompey organised their forces in the other parts of the Empire. Caesar then attempted a surprise attack on an eminence called Puig Bordel that stood unfortified between Gardeny and the town, and again failed in his objective. The following day Fabius's pontoon bridges—one lately restored—were both swept away in a new flood and for ten days Caesar's troops were on short rations while a convoy of supplies from Gaul, which arrived during this period, was in real danger, despite its strong escort of Gallic cavalry, until Caesar, availing himself of his experiences in Britain, got a coracle service going across the river and, in the end, a new pontoon built in the face of much enemy interference, some miles upstream.

Once the situation was restored, however, the initiative passed to Caesar, who was now far superior in cavalry and thus able to interfere effectively with the lines of communications of the Pompeians: the latter, therefore, in furtherance of their policy of delay, decided to withdraw south of the Ebro and began to bridge that river at Octagesa (Ribarroja) 40 kms. to the south-south-west. In the meantime Caesar had actually been diverting part of the river above the town in order to make a ford for his cavalry.

So on the night of June 1st-2nd the Pompeians began their retreat; Caesar's cavalry forded the river and, at their own request, the legions bravely followed them wading chest deep through the water. The following afternoon they caught up with their enemies, who had been hampered by repeated cavalry attacks and, after a week of manœuvring, compelled them by the prospect of starvation to surrender near the village of Mayalo, still some ten or a dozen kilometres short of their new bridge over the Ebro. The other two Pompeian legions in the south, after this, yielded to the inevitable and by the end of September Caesar was on his way back to receive the surrender of Marseilles. Spain had fallen to him more speedily and at less cost than he could possibly have hoped.

The successes of this year, however, proved illusory, and four years later he had to return to fight and win the battle of Munda, the last of his career, within a comparatively short distance of the place where he had fought his first sixteen years before. For the need to return at all, he had largely to thank Quintus Cassius Longinus, the man that he left in charge of Further Spain. The great commanders of history have seldom been well served by their lieutenants. It is possible that by the fact of their own genius they are unable to create the conditions that can produce other leaders of ability. Certain it is that Caesar was ill served by his: the ablest of them, Labienus, a name familiar to schoolboys from the Gallic War Commentaries, was counted among the enemy dead at Munda.

But the behaviour of Cassius was such as to reflect seriously upon the wisdom of Caesar in giving him the appointment at all. Already possessed of an unsavoury reputation as a financial officer in the same province under the Pompeian régime of 54 B.C., now that he was vested with final authority, Cassius lost no time in sating his most predatory instincts: with the result that within six months not only was he fortunate to survive an attempt on his life in his headquarters at Cordoba, but shortly afterwards, when on his way to Malaga to cross to Africa to join Caesar there, he was deserted by the larger proportion of his troops and compelled to seek refuge in the well-fortified town of

Ulia (Montemayor, near Montilla). From here he was rescued by Lepidus, the governor of Hither Spain, who later became a member of the second Triumvirate formed after Caesar's death. Cassius, his term of office now over, left Malaga by sea and lost his life when his ship foundered in a storm off the mouth of the Ebro.

Such a situation was virtually an open invitation for the Pompeians to intervene, and this they duly did in the following year, 47 B.C. Pompey himself was dead, not having survived by many weeks the crushing defeat at Pharsalus in Greece. But his two sons, Cnaeus and Sextus, were still carrying on the fight, with strong support in North Africa: so, still having command of the sea, Cnaeus crossed to the Balearic Islands and received the surrender of the two larger and took Ibiza by storm. After a short delay caused by illness, he crossed to Cartagena. Meanwhile, the Roman troops in Spain had forestalled his arrival by expelling Cassius's successor, Trebonius, and so, with Caesar's attentions engaged in Alexandria, the two young Pompeys—for Sextus soon joined his elder brother—were free to consolidate their position.

Caesar's victory at Thapsus in the April of 46 B.C. decided the fate of North Africa, but it did eventually, through the aggregation of the defeated remnants, add to the number of his enemies in Spain. Fabius and Pedius were despatched with troops from Rome to stop the rot, but were not able to make any impression: for the forces of the Pompeians amounted to some thirteen legions, with 6,000 cavalry and a like number of auxiliaries. These troops were not all of front-line quality, but even if the elder Pompey was known to be no Sertorius, they represented formidable opposition and it may be a measure of Caesar's anxiety that he should feel constrained to leave Rome in November, in the face of winter, and to make such speed as to cover the 1,500 kms. overland between there and Saguntum in seventeen days.

By the time he arrived in the Guadalquivir valley a fortnight later he had at his command eight legions (four of them seasoned troops) and 8,000 cavalry. The position with which he was confronted was a difficult one: of all the towns in the valley only Ulia (Montemayor) was holding out for him: and his first task was to get reinforcements into it by making a feint attack on Sextus Pompey in Cordoba and drawing Cnaeus away from the siege of it. Then he set about individual towns in order to entice Pompey into a decisive engagement, but the latter for a time evaded the issue and on February 19th abandoned Ategua (Teba la Vieja, on the north bank of the river Guadajon, just north of Osuna on the Seville-Antequera road) and Ventipa (15 kms. to the south-east) at the cost of some decline in the morale of his troops. A month later, on March 17th, a perfect spring day found Pompey drawn up on high ground east of the town of Munda (some 25 kms. south of Ategua) and Caesar's forces crossing the small stream of Carchena and advancing up the slope from the north. Almost in a spirit of bravado, Pompey decided to accept the challenge.

The fighting was long and bitter: two hours of charge and countercharge went by with the adverse slope counterbalancing the sounder training of Caesar's infantry: his cavalry, however, superior in quantity as well as in quality, had driven their opposite numbers from the field and had been recalled and were being held in reserve. In the end the famous X Legion cracked the enemy's left and the cavalry were ordered back into the fight to press home the advantage from flank and rear. Victory for the Caesarians was now inevitable, but it was hastened by an error. The hard-pressed Pompeians mistook the movement of their own troops, who were being transferred to deal with the new situation, as the beginning of a general retreat and within a trice the fighting was over.

Not so the slaughter, however: exhausted by the long struggle that in the end had gone against them, the Pompeians were in no condition even to escape; they were rounded up and cut down in their thousands. An eyewitness gives a macabre account of how a wall of dead bodies was built round the town of Munda and heads were set on stakes to stare, unseeing, mock sentries on a wall of flesh.

Cnaeus Pompey fled from the scene of carnage to his naval base at Carteia (near Algeciras), but was eventually tracked down and killed, and his head put on view for the citizens of Cordoba on April 13th. His brother Sextus escaped detection altogether and lived to fight another day. The dissident cities of the south surrendered one by one, Cordoba, Hispalis (Seville), Urso (Osuna) and Munda itself: in each the inflamed passions of a civil war took their human toll. But even if Caesar was in no mood to revive his gentler treatment of four years before, he was not entirely destructive. The faithful Ulia and Cartagena, Tarragona and Celsa (on the Ebro) were all raised to the level of 'coloniae' with full citizen status: some land was taken from Hispalis (Seville) and Urso (Osuna) and other towns in the district to provide for the settlement of demobilised soldiers. In fact, in the short time left to him, Caesar began the Romanisation of the south of Spain that it was one of Augustus's finest achievements to complete.

CHAPTER VI

Spain under Augustus, the First Emperor

SPAIN was mercifully spared a major part in the disturbances that followed Caesar's death on the Ides of March of 44 B.C. It is true that Sextus Pompeius emerged from his hiding-place in the Eastern Pyrenees with sufficient followers to move south and enter Cartagena; but Lepidus, who was again governor of Hither Spain, came to an arrangement with him whereby the latter proceeded to Sicily, where opportunities for more effective intervention in the new civil war were known to exist: this was in November 44 B.C. Lepidus stayed in control, first of his own province, later of both, until after the battle of Philippi in the autumn of 42 B.C., where it is interesting to note that a mixed force of 6,000 Lusitanian and Iberian cavalry fought on the losing side. Then, under a fresh redistribution of provinces among the Triumvirate, Lepidus was moved to Africa, and Spain left to the young Octavius, who did not take charge in person, but sent a deputy.

Later at the end of 40 B.C. Octavius ceded Spain to Lucius Antonius, brother of the third Triumvir, Marcus, and he, in his turn, despatched deputies: so, never meriting the personal attentions of the great, Spain continued all through the thirties a virtual spectator of the great issues decided in the East, until in 31 B.C. the battle of Actium brought victory for the West and an imperial throne for Octavius, who soon emerged as the first Emperor Augustus. A new régime, however, was but an invitation for those Spaniards not directly assimilated into either Roman province to assert their claims for full independence. In 26 B.C. Augustus came to Spain to direct operations in what has become known as the Cantabrian War. While the presence of the Emperor himself may be some indication of the importance attached to it, at the same time six triumphs during the proceeding ten years for Roman generals operating in the north and north-west of the Peninsula would suggest that some 'softening-up' process had been going on.

However that may be, soon after his arrival in Spain, the Emperor moved north from his base at Segisama (Sasamon, to the west of Burgos) and defeated the Cantabrians in a battle at Vellica some 60 kms. to the north. Three columns were operating against the Galicians, Asturians and Cantabrians respectively: by the end of the year the centre column had forced its way through to the sea, near modern Santander via Juliobriga (near Reinosa) and was thereafter maintained in the rear of the enemies by supplies brought in by sea from south-west Gaul.

With the end of the campaigning season, Augustus, worn out and ill, returned to Tarragona, where he stayed the whole of the next year. In 25 B.C., no longer under the handicap of an ailing commander, the Roman forces campaigned vigorously: one force pushed past Leon and Astorga over the Montanas de Leon into the upper Sil valley and, joined from the south-west by a second force, beleaguered the Asturians on a height called Mons Medullius (probably the mountain St. Julian, near Tuy on the river Miño) and with the eventual reduction of this strong point brought the war ostensibly to a successful end. Augustus left for Rome early in 24 B.C. and gave official sanction to the proclamation of peace throughout the Empire. Nevertheless, the sternest measures were still necessary to suppress the Cantabrians, and Marcus Agrippa, Augustus's 'strong man', had to be present in person to see them applied. Only in the year 19 B.C. can the long process of the conquest of Spain that had started almost exactly two hundred years before be fairly described as ended.

The contrast between this and the swift conquest of Gaul raises interesting considerations. In the first place, the Gauls were organised into much larger, and therefore fewer, tribes: victories over them were likely to be more decisive: France, too, was a land where, for the most part, armies could live comfortably: in Spain large forces could barely maintain themselves and small forces tended to be wiped out by guerilla activities. But, even so, when all due allowance has been made, tribute must be paid to the tenacity and courage of the native Spaniards.

Augustus was nothing if not a tactful peacemaker: the system of dyarchy which he had devised, whereby the old forms of republican government—senate, consuls, praetors and the like—were retained, while those provinces that required to be manned by troops were put under the control of the emperor, was applied to Spain. As early as 27 B.C. there was a scheme for the redistribution of the Peninsula into three provinces. But it can scarcely have been put into practice until after hostilities ceased some eight years later. Then

Further Spain was shorn of the land west of the Guadiana, and this latter, combined with what is now modern Portugal south of the Douro, became the new province of Lusitania, a title that, one likes to think, was a belated tribute to the valiant people who had so resolutely and for so long defended their freedom.

The remnant of Further Spain, now comprising little more than the Baetis (Guadalquivir) river basin, became known as Baetica, with Cordoba as its capital, whilst the rest of the country—far the larger proportion—retained its title of Hither Spain or Tarraconensis—after its capital Tarragona. Under the new system, Lusitania and Tarraconensis, requiring the presence of troops, were imperial provinces and were governed by 'legati' appointed directly by the emperor himself: the legate of Tarraconensis had three subordinate legates to help him govern his huge territory, one for Galicia and Asturias with two legions, one for Cantabria, with one legion based on Reinosa, and a third for the rest with no troops.

The three provinces were further subdivided into smaller units (conventus) for the administration of justice: in Tarraconensis there were seven such, based on Cartagena, Tarragona, Saragossa, Clunia (Coruña del Conde), Astorga, Lugo and Braga (in Portugal); in Lusitania three, round Pax Julia (Beja in Portugal), Scallabis (Santaren on the Tagus north of Lisbon) and Augusta Emerita (Merida) the new provincial capital, founded by the Emperor himself for the retirement of those of his veterans who had served under him in the Cantabrian War. Baetica had four, based on Cadiz, Cordoba, Seville and Ecija: while it is obvious that such detailed organisation as this was not the work of a single day any more than the building of Rome itself, it is equally clear that the Romanisation of Spain was being pushed with considerable vigour. Britain, to the end of her Roman days, never had more than four coloniae (i.e. centres of population that were entirely Roman either by emigration of civilians or settlement of veterans); Spain soon had twenty-three.[1] Not all were new colonies, but neither do they represent all the new towns of this date. New urban centres such as Lugo and Astorga appeared in the north-west as prospective tribal centres for the latest additions to the empire of Rome.

A start was also made at this period to foster the growth of provincial councils (concilia) in connection with the new cult of emperor-worship. These bodies, of ill-defined constitution, had mainly a ritualistic-cum-social function, approximating roughly to the Masonic movement of our own times. A priest (flamen) was elected and the office was greatly coveted. Councils might stage games in the provincial capital, when they assembled, and messages were sent direct to the emperor on such occasions as his birthday. But this interesting contact with the chief executive of the State was never developed further, although on very rare occasions complaints about the conduct of provincial governors were made through this channel. Tarragona almost certainly had a 'concilium' before Augustus died; Baetica had one by A.D. 25 and Lusitania followed suit. Subsidiary to these 'concilia' and at a lower

[1] Barcino (Barcelona), Tarragona, Valentia, Zaragossa, Celsa (Velilla del Ebro), Libisosa (Lezuza, west of Albacete), Salaria (Ubeda la Vieja, east of Linares), Tortosa, Clunia (Coruña del Conde, south-east of Burgos), Acci (Guadix, east of Granada), Ilici (Elche south-west of Alicante), Metellinum (Medellin, east of Merida), Norva (Caceres), Merida, Italica (Santiponce, near Seville), Carteia (near Algeciras), Hasta Regia (near Jerez), Urso (Osuna), Itucci (near Baena), Ucubi (Espejo, south-east of Cordoba), Seville, Astigi (Ecija, south-west of Cordoba) and Tucci (Martos, west of Jaen).

social level were the 'Seviri Augustales', a priesthood open to freedmen (liberti) who were often men of substance. Both systems lasted well into the third century.

Hand in hand with the building of new towns or the re-furbishing of old ones, went the construction of roads. The building of a major road was no light matter, for they were intended to last: the foundations were laid some 2 feet below ground level and four layers of stone were needed to complete the job. First the existing Via Maxima that had been started before 120 B.C., leading from the eastern Pyrenees round the coast to Cadiz, was repaired and renamed the Via Augusta. Other major roads followed: from Tarragona to the far north-west via Lerida, Saragossa to Astorga and Lugo, with side roads, from Lerida to Huesca; from Saragossa, one to Jaca, a second to Pamplona and the Basque coast at Oyarzun. From Astorga a major road ran south through Zamora, Salamanca, and Caceres to Merida: another linked Merida with Saragossa through Toledo, Alcala de Henares and Siguenza: a third led from Merida to Cordoba via Medellin and round to Antequera and Malaga; a fourth joined Merida with Cadiz, passing through Seville, with a branch road left through Ecija to Antequera and a second on the right to the tin mines and Huelva. Indeed, every mining district was well served by roads, since their construction was as much dictated by commercial as by military interests.

For with the establishment of the Empire and the disappearance from the world of major wars, economic development became possible: and in any such development, Spain, with her rich mineral resources, was bound to figure prominently. Gold, silver, copper, lead, tin and iron began to be mined in increasing amounts. Most of the gold was found in Asturias, but in other parts also, in smaller quantities: silver came from Almaden (Sisapo) and the extensive workings in the neighbourhood of Cartagena; copper from the Rio Tinto, iron from the Cantabrian hills. Under the Republic, such mines as were at that time in action were run mainly as private enterprises, with the owners having little but the right of conquest with which to justify their ownership.

This system prevailed until the early days of the Empire, when all mines became State property, by the process of purchase, inheritance or confiscation; gold mines first, then silver, then the rest. They were then farmed out again to private individuals or companies, with the result that private enterprise was restored, saddled now, however, by the prepayment of a substantial 'royalty' to the imperial treasury. But State-owned or not, the mines were mainly dependent on slave labour for their working. Lead and tin were exported as far afield as India, whilst iron was particularly welcome in Italy.

Nor was this the limit of Spain's productivity: dyes from Baetica and elsewhere are mentioned; esparto grass for cordwaining was grown in the district north of Cartagena; linen yarns from Galicia and linen fabrics from Emporiae and Tarragona were the best obtainable anywhere. Much raw wool was exported from Baetica, and Salacia (Alcacer-do-Sal in Portugal) was well known for its finished woollen goods. Food and drink figured in the lists as well. Spanish wines and olive oil were able to compete in Italian markets, Tarragona and the Balearic Islands being prominent with the former. Baetica was one of the corn granaries of Rome, and her artichokes are mentioned as finding favour with epicures, whilst Malaga did a good trade in salted fish. Cadiz, Tarragona and Cartagena, in that order, waxed prosperous as the ports through which most of this trade passed, the first-named in particular, true to its Phoenician origin, being the leading 'business' city of Spain. Early in the first century, in fact, Strabo calls it the second city of the empire.

Strabo was a native of Cappadocia in Asia Minor, who, writing in Greek, by about the year 6 B.C. had completed his seventeen books of geographical survey of the Mediterranean countries. The third book is devoted to the Iberian Peninsula and, although it was one of the countries of the west that he had never visited, so much of what he says in it is corroborated from other sources, that the whole of it can be accepted with reasonable confidence.

He mentions the natural features, the rivers, the mountains, the tides—he is particularly intrigued by the Atlantic tides beyond the Pillars of Hercules—he describes where each of the main tribal communities lived, he mentions the mines and lists the exports: he contrasts the beauty and fertility of the south with the barrenness of the north. Whereas the Turdetani have become almost completely Romanised and, therefore, he implies, civilised, the Cantabrians sleep on the ground, grow their hair long like women, eat goats' meat and make bread from acorns; they drink water or beer, but not wine, and cook with butter in place of olive oil: their sick they expose, as the Assyrians did and for the same reason—namely, that they might receive attention from those who had recovered from the same illness: their wildness and intractability, says Strabo, were largely due to their remoteness; now that the Romans are in charge, the situation in general is beginning to improve. He pays a tribute to the fighting qualities of the Lusitanians, describing their weapons and equipment, and finds that a section of them who lived near the Douro river were like the Spartans in their fondness for bathing and in their restraint at meals; they were adept at guerrilla warfare and ambushes, and were splendid horsemen over rough country, with well-trained mounts.

Wild horses were native to the country, he observes, as were also deer, and the horses were speedier than those of the Parthians in the east, and smoother runners: amongst the bird life of the country are mentioned swans and bustards; and crows, which his authority, Posidonius, had been surprised to find black. Beavers inhabited the rivers, but the castor from them had no medicinal qualities. Two other animals were present in such numbers as to assume the proportions of a plague. The first was the rabbit. The Greeks, for once, not having a word for it, a rabbit was described as a burrowing hare, or, expressively, as a 'peeler'. Rabbits infested the whole country and beyond, as far as Marseilles, and the Balearic Islands as well: indeed, the inhabitants of these latter had, on one occasion, been constrained to approach the Romans to ask for somewhere else to live: nothing seems to have come of the request. Strabo refers to some of the remedial measures adopted, which included the importation of ferrets from Libya, but he is mistaken in thinking that ferrets drag rabbits out of their warrens. The second menace was the rat, and this particularly applied to the Cantabrian hills, where the Romans were hard put to it to eke out the grain supplies, in spite of the special terms that were offered to rat-catchers, and were often compelled to import additional grain over the rough tracks that led from France.

The wearing of the mantilla by Spanish women is obviously a survival from pre-Roman days. 'Other women', writes Strabo, 'put a rod about a foot high on the head, twist their hair round the rod and then drape it with a dark veil.' Not so, apparently, the 'paseo', that informal evening stroll, so universal throughout modern Spain. 'When the members of a local tribe visited a Roman camp for the first time, and saw Roman officers promenading up and down merely for the sake of exercise, they supposed them to be crazy and tried to induce them to return to their tents, thinking that they should either remain quietly seated or else be fighting.'

The recent Civil War in Spain provided on both sides many instances of that particular form of courage that amounts almost to a contempt for pain and an insensibility to death. It was a quality present to a high degree in the ancient Iberians. In describing the inevitable tortures inflicted upon the assassin of Hasdrubal in 221 B.C., Livy says that the victim bore an ineffaceable smile upon his face throughout. In the Cantabrian Wars of the third decade B.C. mothers killed their children before being taken prisoner: and even a small boy, whose parents and brothers were in fetters as prisoners of war, gained possession of a sword and, at the command of his father, killed them all. Other prisoners, nailed to a cross, sang a paean of victory. In the same context, it can be added that it was an Iberian custom that those who had devoted themselves to the service of a master should not survive the death of that master, but die by a poison traditionally prepared from a kind of wild parsley. This was a trait of which the Roman generals and emperors, from Sertorius onwards, were not slow to take advantage.

Merida. Theatre, showing remains of portico behind the stage

Merida. Theatre seen from the main entrance

CHAPTER VII

Spain under the Early Empire

EVENTS and developments in Spain of normal historical interest after the death of Augustus in A.D. 14 are few and far between, and the reason for this is not far to seek. The country had received a final settlement under Augustus, and it is clear that there was much wisdom and virtue in it. But above all the geographical position of Spain, tucked away in the west, was an effective guarantee of no interference from without. The Atlantic Ocean and, to a lesser degree, the Pyrenees, were an effective *cordon sanitaire*. Spain could have none of the frontier troubles of the Rhine, the Danube and the east.

But even in Spain, there were changes: peace was not synonymous with stagnation. The Emperor Claudius (A.D. 41-58) restored to Tarraconensis the districts of Galicia and Asturias that, possibly, his predecessor Tiberius included in Lusitania, and emphasised his interest in that part of the world by founding the town of Claudiomerium a few miles east of Cape Finisterre.

In the year A.D. 68, on the death of Nero, the armies of Rome demonstrated that they were the real power behind the imperial throne by appointing between them four successive emperors within a single year.

E

Spain was first in the news because the first nomination was the elderly and respected Galba, who had been in charge of the imperial province of Tarraconensis for some eight years. A proclamation to this effect was duly made in Cartagena on April 2nd, and it received the support of Marcus Otho, the governor of the other imperial Spanish province, Lusitania.

But, as the empire's chief administrator, Galba proved sadly disappointing, even in the short time given to him. He was slow in reaching Rome and did not arrive there until the autumn. At one stage he had retired to the comparative obscurity of Clunia (Coruña del Conde) and had even contemplated suicide there as an end for his confusion. However, in the following January he was unceremoniously removed from the scene by the above-mentioned Otho, who had recourse to assassination, when Galba failed to nominate him as heir to the principate. Spain's direct participation, in any sense, in the exciting events of this year, ended when Otho shortly succumbed to Vitellius, commander of the troops on the northern frontier. Before the year was out, Vespasian arrived from the East at the head of his troops and, with all rivals eliminated, established himself as the first of the Flavian Emperors.

Under the Flavians (A.D. 69-96) there was considerable economic development in Spain rendered necessary by the dwindling returns from the mines of Greece and Asia Minor. While Asturias and Galicia still remained as the main sources of gold, the rivers Tagus and Douro were now yielding a considerable quota of their own. By the end of the first century A.D. the production of gold was running at the high figure of 20,000 lb. per year, that of silver at more than 8 tons.

Known mineral resources were developed and new ones prospected: silver from Castulo (Cazlona) was added to the already large yield of the mines near Cartagena: lead was often a secondary product of silver mines, but, in any case, it was extensively mined, under its own right, in both Cantabria and Baetica: much copper passed through Cordoba, down-river, to the outer world, from new workings at the western end of the Sierra Morena. Fresh deposits of iron ore were discovered on the east coast near Dianium (Denia) to supplement the older ones of Cantabria.

A few towns, among them Toletum (Toledo) and Bilbilis (Catalayud on the Madrid-Saragossa highway) were beginning to avail themselves of properties in their local water supply to produce finished steel goods. The only mines known by the Roman world to yield mercury and cinnabar were at Sisapo (Almaden), on the border of Tarraconensis and Baetica, and to complete an impressive list, tin was mined in both Galicia and Lusitania. With the exception, mentioned above, of some finished steel goods, all these metals passed from Spain as raw materials—in the form of ingots, where this was possible—for the workshops of Italy and elsewhere. On the other hand, quarries that produced materials for tiles and bricks were barely numerous enough to supply native Spanish needs: from the marble quarries of Mons Marianus, however, there may have been from time to time an exportable surplus.

Equally noticeable, too, compared with the Augustan period, was the development of those products best summarised under the heading of agricultural. The olive tree, first introduced into the south of Spain by the Phoenicians, had already spread to the limits in which it is still found today—namely, in the east and west coastal regions, in the valleys of the Ebro, Guadalquivir and the Douro and on the central plateau, south of the Guadarramas: olive oil from Spain was becoming increasingly valuable in Italy towards the end of the first century A.D. as local supplies began to prove inadequate for the needs of a growing population.

The growing of wheat had likewise been greatly extended: previously confined to the Guadalquivir basin, it had now spread to all parts of the Peninsula except the extreme north, where the rainfall made it an unprofitable experiment. It must not be imagined, however, that the high plateaux, north and south of the Guadarramas, were, in Roman times, one large, waving cornfield: aridity then, as now, must have been a limiting factor, and such wheat as was produced there was always light-weight compared with that of the lower-lying Andalusia. Yet a mosaic of this time, unearthed at Ostia, the port of Rome, lists Spain with Sicily, Egypt and Africa as the chief corn-producing provinces of the Empire: and in the absence of meat in general, and of most common vegetables, bread figured very prominently in the diet of the ancient world. Even so, as population increased throughout the Mediterranean world, there were occasions when the Empire narrowly escaped the peril of starvation.

Nor were minerals and food Spain's only exports: from the earliest stages of their acquaintance with them, the Romans had been quick to realise that the Spaniards had the necessary qualities to make good soldiers both as horse and foot. During the first century A.D. many of the garrison troops doing duty in the north of Spain were native Spaniards recruited indiscriminately from the three provinces: as many more were serving abroad on the Rhine and elsewhere.

Many auxiliary corps of the Roman army bore Spanish names. Lusitania and Tarraconensis regularly shared with Germany the honour of supplying personnel for the Emperor's praetorian bodyguard.

However, in the course of time, as the country became no longer directly involved in wars owing to its safe geographical position in the west, the military qualities of its inhabitants became less pronounced and the Emperor Hadrian (A.D. 117-137), himself a Spaniard, expressed some displeasure on this account. Nevertheless, this decline did mean that fewer troops were needed for the garrisoning of the Peninsula. Even by the time of Nero (A.D. 58-68) the three legions prescribed for the purpose by Augustus had dwindled to one. Despite the turbulence of the intervening year, Vespasian (A.D. 69-79) saw no need to increase this number. It was he, in fact, who transferred the VII Legion from Pannonia in the Balkans to what appears to have been a new camp at Leon: the name Leon is a derivative of the single 'Legio' that gave the town its origin.

It was Vespasian, too, who decisively affected Spain on the political and civil side by the award of 'jus Italicum' or Latin rights to all the free people of Spain who were not already full Roman citizens. These Latin rights virtually constituted Roman citizenship of the second class. It was a distinction that had existed from the early days of the Republic, at a time when the city of Rome was acquiring mastery over the neighbouring cities of Latium. But in the provinces it was a distinction that, in practice, did not make a deal of difference: for Latin rights conferred upon a man all the personal privileges of a full citizen: and the fact that he was still unable to vote or hold office in Rome was of little consequence to a Spaniard who was never likely to go there. But it was of enormous benefit for him to know that he had legal protection against the arbitrary violence of magistrates and of others: that he could do business anywhere in the world with the certainty that his contracts would be recognised and defended by Roman law.

At this stage, when two Spaniards are in turn, about to occupy—and occupy with distinction—the imperial throne, it is not inappropriate briefly to review the development of the relations between Roman and Spaniard. Under the Republic, during the long years of conquest, the Romans undoubtedly looked upon the Spaniards as barbarians and savages; as indeed they were (save for a fringe on the south and east coasts), in comparison, at least, with the Greeks, with whom first-hand acquaintance was simultaneously being made. This disdain would be particularly marked in the educated class of Rome, as it was on them that the Greek way of life made the strongest impression and, at that stage in the history of the Republic, the educated class still largely retained control of policy-making. It is, perhaps, significant that Cato the Elder, who so vehemently opposed the introduction of Greek refinements into Italy, was always sympathetic in his attitude to the Spaniards. Possibly, therefore, it is the divergence in methods of approach towards east and west that explains, but is far from excusing, the many instances of bad faith that the Romans showed towards the Spaniards in the second century B.C.

Correspondingly, however, Spain may be said to have reaped a benefit when, on the establishment of the Empire after 31 B.C., Augustus tried to bring about by every means of propaganda at his disposal the moral regeneration of his people. In any campaign for a return to the simpler virtues of the past, the more primitive west would tend to attract more attention than the decadent east, and it is certainly a fact that, under Augustus, unusual attention was paid to the material development of Spain. Thereafter, the vast amount of trading that ensued between Rome and Spain rendered the Spanish accent in spoken Latin, with its occasional archaisms, as familiar and acceptable in the influential strata of Roman society as is the accent of Scotland in London society.

Nevertheless, it was only a small percentage of middle- and upper-class Spaniards who gained any direct contact with Rome and the Romans. It was only in the towns of Andalusia, the east coast and the Ebro valley that there was any marked transition to Roman manners and the Roman way of life, in the first century A.D. The great contrast between city and country that is so noticeable in modern Spain, must have existed then. The loyalty of the non-urban population was still given to the tiniest territorial unit of their tribal organisation, and the Roman government never did completely succeed in destroying this parochialism and substituting in the minds of its adherents the feeling that they were members of a world-wide Empire.

The mining districts of the hills were always rough and barbarous, although here the people concerned were mainly slaves: for mines were almost invariably staffed—up to and including the level of foreman—by slaves, and they, often aliens in an alien land, had little encouragement to live other than a brutish existence. Somewhat naturally, the Galicians, Asturians and Cantabrians were stubbornest in resisting the infiltration of culture: indeed, the survival of the Basque language would suggest that in one section of the north, at least, the Latin language never was accepted. Catalan, too, may be another Iberian dialect that survived in the fastnesses of the eastern Pyrenees.

There were few towns at this period that had attained any considerable size: in Tarraconensis, Tarragona itself, Valencia and Barcelona: in Baetica, Cordoba, Seville and Cadiz: in Lusitania, Merida and Lisbon (Olisipo). The number of small towns, comprising two or three thousand inhabitants, was legion, reflecting the efforts made by the Romans to attract local loyalties.

In general, as well as being centres for the dissemination of Roman culture, towns were the instruments of local government. It is obvious that the official governor of a senatorial province or his counterpart in an imperial province, the legatus, could exercise only a general supervision over local affairs. Local business, such as maintenance of order, collection of taxes, control of religious cults and festivals and the upkeep of public buildings was left in the hands of a town council (decuriones), possibly a hundred strong, headed by two mayors (duoviri) on the pattern of the two consuls at Rome, and two aediles who were part surveyors, part police-superintendents. The council was largely composed of *ex-officio* mayors and aediles, and although there was competition for office, because the prize was not only one year of power but also full Roman citizenship for life, it would in practice be confined to the existing ring of decuriones, plus a small amount of recruitment from below, to maintain numbers.

Communications between these many administrative

centres and the outside world had been established by a network of roads planned and partly constructed by the government of Augustus (as already described). Vespasian added his own contribution to the network, mainly to the north and north-west. Thanks to the labours of his VII Legion a new road was built from Astorga to Braga (in northern Portugal): from the Col de Roncevaux to Pamplona and from Brigantium (Coruña) to Iria Flavia (El Padron just south of Santiago de Compostela) a name that reveals the time of its origin. But Vespasian's policy of development and Romanisation was not confined to those communities whose titles reflect his family names. It is estimated that as many as ninety Spanish towns owe to it either their origin or the decisive stage of their growth.

CHAPTER VIII

Spain under the Later Emperors

IT is unfortunate that the advent upon the Imperial throne of the first provincial, a Spaniard, should have coincided with the end of the two-hundred-year period of Latin literature that we call Classical. Anything that was written of the reigns of Trajan (A.D. 98-117) and of Hadrian (119-138) has survived, at best, in fragmentary form. History comes to be based more and more on the evidence of inscription and excavation, less and less on literary records. More evidence of the good things that the two Emperors did for the land of their birth still stands, duly inscribed, rooted in the soil of Spain, than may be gleaned from any literary records that can be found to describe them. Not that everything Roman that is associated with Trajan in common parlance is rightly named: there has been a natural tendency to ascribe otherwise unidentified relics to the best-known name in Hispano-Roman affairs. It is very likely, for instance, that the so-called Arch of Trajan in Merida is no more correctly styled than the cinema in the same town that also bears his name.

Moreover, it will be wrong to see in the many public

works which were erected in Spain during these two reigns a manifestation of sentiment. Between them, the many Emperors of Rome had many faults, but parochial-mindedness was seldom one of them. Trajan and Hadrian, like all the others of their class in the provinces, were Romans first and Spaniards second. Trajan was mainly concerned throughout his reign by war in the east of his own making, and whereas Hadrian quickly reversed the expansionist policy of his predecessor, he was a most assiduous visitor to all the frontiers of his Empire and well-known as an admirer of Greek culture.

Yet undoubtedly the accession to the supreme power of these the first provincials created a new and altogether healthier climate in the imperial court which, for a short while at least, had a salutary effect throughout the entire administration. Particularly is this true of Trajan. As a general, he had never disdained to share the hardships of the men under him and had often been seen marching in their midst, covered with sweat and dust, leading his horse. Now, elected Emperor, he made his first entrance into Rome, not borne in a litter or mounted in a chariot, but on foot, distinguishable among the crowd that thronged around him only by the impressive proportions of his physique. Modest and simple by nature, he was yet astute enough to revive the tactful policy of Augustus and give new life to the old fiction that power was divided between 'princeps' and senate. Small wonder that more than two hundred years later Eutropius can tell us that the Senate was still acclaiming each new Emperor as 'more fortunate than Augustus, more virtuous than Trajan'. Left-handed though it was, the compliment was none the less a real one.

Hadrian too, in his turn, was anxious to continue the good work of his predecessor, and on the evidence of coins he merited—or was given—the title of Restitutor Hispaniae. At any rate, the restoration of the Temple of Augustus at Tarragona and the embellishment of the theatre at Merida are two things that can be accounted to his credit. But the economic crisis that caused him swiftly to drop Trajan's policy of expansion was a sharp one; and Spain did not escape its consequences, as is revealed by the fact that as early in the reign as A.D. 118 the Treasury had to forgo certain dues owed by her, in common with many other provinces. Simultaneously the need for troops of better quality was becoming apparent. The recruitment of new Emperors from the provinces had not been a mere accident, but rather the final acknowledgment of declining standards all through Italy. In a conference at Tarragona in A.D. 120 Hadrian himself discussed the problem with prominent men from the three Spanish provinces and took the occasion to reproach his fellow countrymen with their reluctance to undertake military service, which, since the time of the Flavians, no longer involved leaving the Peninsula.

This century, the second of our era, is widely accepted as having been the happiest and most successful of any for the Roman Empire of the west. But long before the end of it, defences were proved to be woefully inadequate even in safe Spain, when in A.D. 170 large numbers of pirates from Africa, making light of the official garrison there, crossed the Straits and sacked Malaga, destroying its citadel, and proceeded to lay siege to Singilis (Antequera la Vieja). Baetica, being a senatorial province, had no troops at all, and the beleaguered town was not relieved until Maximinus, governor of the nearby Imperial province of Lusitania, arrived with hastily assembled troops; nor did the raiders deign to return whence they came, until Varius Clemens, with a fleet, threatened to cut off their retreat. As a consequence of this alarming and significant event, Baetica was declared to be an Imperial province and a detachment of the VII Legion was posted in Italica.

Yet quite apart from external causes of this sort, there had been financial difficulties in the province. In 1888 there was discovered in Seville an inscription containing a senatorial decree, issued on the initiative of the Emperor Marcus Aurelius (A.D. 161-180) reducing the total amount of dues to be paid. Under the cruder and less flexible structure of Roman finance, it may be assumed that tax-reduction was never a sign of increasing prosperity, but only a *de facto* recognition of the inability of the poor tax-payer to produce the statutory amount.

The two greatest menaces to the existence of the Empire were barbaric invasion from outside and dissension from within. Even under the Antonines, whose name is so closely associated with the Empire's best days, the first had occasioned the so-called Marcomannic War in the area of the Danube: the second, bred of the first, was not long delayed. In A.D. 187 an Italian adventurer called Maternus gathered together a large irregular force in a manner that recalled Spartacus and the last disorderly decades of the dying Republic, and careered through Gaul and Spain, leaving a trail of havoc in his wake until his movement perished of its own inanition. Like some baleful comet, it was an omen of things to come.

The violent death of the Emperor Commodus in

A.D. 192 plunged the state into civil war, and Spain, for a while, found it expedient to espouse the cause of the nominee of the legions in Britain, one Clodius Albinus, an African, but was not unduly involved when he fell a victim near Lyons to his rival and fellow African, Severus, A.D. 197.

The third century early brought an administrative change in the Peninsula with the formation of Galicia and Asturias together into a separate province. But this purely domestic rearrangement was soon eclipsed in importance by Caracalla's action in extending full Roman citizenship to all members of the Empire in the first year of his reign (A.D. 211-217). This marked the culmination of the policy first devised by Julius Caesar, started by Augustus so cautiously and later so notably advanced by Vespasian. The final step, however, was almost certainly taken from motives that did not tally precisely with those that occasioned the first one. Beyond doubt, Caracalla hoped that his action would promote a sense of unity throughout his Empire against invasions from without. Obviously, also, administration was made much simpler and easier by the change. But whereas in the time of Augustus citizenship was a privilege to be jealously guarded, by the time of Caracalla it involved financial liabilities. For the wheel had gone full circle since those days long ago in 167 B.C. when, with the influx of slaves and wealth from the newly-won conquests, Roman citizens had been declared virtually free of taxes: now an extension of the franchise meant an increase in revenue for the Imperial Treasury.

Obviously the new Constitution—for the extension of the franchise was no less—was an important landmark in the history of the Spanish provinces. All peculiarities and anomalies in local government disappeared: hundreds of towns that even after the time of Vespasian with their 'Latin rights' had enjoyed no higher status than that of foreign communities federated with Rome, were now fully integrated into the Roman system. Even more important, perhaps, was the granting of citizenship to those many who still lived in the countryside and had not yet been organised into any local community. A stroke of the pen, so to speak, however momentous, was not likely to cause them to abandon to any marked degree a mode of life that was still largely tribal, but it did mean that from now on there was little political advantage to be gained from urban life, and the development of large country estates that was so prominent a feature throughout western Europe in the latter days of the Empire may well have received its original impulse from the realisation of that fact.

It was under the same Caracalla that, in the field of foreign affairs, the German menace was revived for the first time in two hundred years: so effective had been the work of Julius Caesar and Augustus. In fact, Caracalla dealt with the situation admirably, and it was not until the second half of the century that Spain was involved. By then, along with Britain, Spain was under the control of the usurper Postumus, who succeeded in maintaining for ten years or so from A.D. 260 a Gallic Empire of the west in defiance of the real Emperor Gallienus, who was occupied in dealing with the Gothic invasion of the Balkan Peninsula. Truth to tell, Rome was hard put to it at this period to survive, and this involuntary division of command was a precedent for the official cleavage of the Empire into East and West that was soon to follow.

Postumus's defence of his own frontiers against the barbarians can only have been intermittently successful, because it was during his decade of supremacy in the West that the Suebi and Franks succeeded in reaching Spain. Tarragona was the chief sufferer: in the process of being beleaguered and captured by the invaders, she sustained such a vast amount of damage that signs of it were still visible two centuries later. Modern Barcelona owes its pre-eminence as the largest city of the north-east to the fact that the Roman Barcino was selected for further development before the provincial capital had recovered from this crippling blow. Further down the coast the port of Dianium (Denia) was laid in ruins in the same invasion, and at Emporiae (Ampurias) the abandonment during this period of that section of the town that was of Greek foundation is almost certainly a consequence of the activities of these same enemies.

Shortly afterwards, with the accession of Diocletian (A.D. 284-305), in an effort to put a stop to the anarchy into which the Empire was beginning to slip, the office of Emperor was converted into a despotism in the Eastern manner. One result was that all provinces were now imperial ones and none was any longer run by the Senate. The creation of the separate province of Galicia, under Caracalla, has already been mentioned. Not long afterwards, part of the north African province of Mauretania—namely, Tingitana (Tangier)—was declared to be a Spanish province. This would imply that communications between Rome and what is modern Morocco were better through Spain than by any other route, and in any event it is interesting to note that Spain's direct connection with North Africa begins at this early date.

Memorial to the Atilian family at Sadaba

Tomb at Fabara in the lower Ebro Valley

Now, under Diocletian, in step with the decline in the fortunes of its capital city, the province of Tarraconensis itself was split into two and the southern half, being based on Nova Carthago (Cartagena) received the title of Carthaginiensis. Apart from the award of provincial status to the Balearic Islands in A.D. 404, this was the last change in administration affecting the Peninsula. Each province received its governor by nomination from the Emperor and the governors, in their turn, were under the supervision of a special representative of the Emperor, who resided in Hispalis (Seville), then the largest city in Spain.

The name of Diocletian is, of course, primarily associated with the first official decision to split the Empire into two halves. Diocletian himself took the eastern half and made his capital at Nicomedia while, to avoid possible complications that Rome, as the other capital, might create, Milan was selected as the headquarters of the co-Emperor Maximianus. This arrangement, however, was short-lived: for the next Emperor, Constantine, proclaimed in York in A.D. 306, made it his business to restore the unity of the Empire once more and in the end, shortly before his death in A.D. 337, reversed the religious policy of his predecessor also by accepting Christianity as the religion of the State.

This, the final triumph of Christianity over the ancient gods of Rome, was further proof of the growing preponderance of the East over the West. The transference of the seat of political power to the newly-erected capital of Constantinople had been of a significance that no one could mistake. The West, and with it Spain in particular, was in undoubted decline. Owing to its proximity to the frontier of the Rhine,

Gaul surpassed Spain in importance, and this fact was recognised by Constantine when he made the Spanish provinces dependencies of the newly-styled Prefecture of Gaul.

By the very nature of its beliefs, Christianity was bound to be disruptive in its effect upon the Roman State. The Roman State, fundamentally, was a slave State, and to such a state Christian beliefs were essentially opposed. It may be no concern of this book to offer an exhaustive study of the reasons that led to the fall of a great Empire, but it is directly concerned with some nine millions of its inhabitants, and these can scarcely be consigned to outer darkness with no greater interest in their fate than that conveyed by a bare recital of facts.

During the long years of territorial expansion, and for a long time after the boundaries were static, the economy of Rome had been cushioned against shocks by the plentiful supply of cheap slave-labour. This condition had had a particularly harmful effect on the development of technical skills. In the palmy days, the answer to the need for larger constructional jobs, for instance, was not the discovery of new techniques, but the direction of even more hands to use the old ones. Consequently, technical development was virtually at a standstill. Whereas the Romans entered upon their Empire with an ample lead over all possible opponents in weapons of war, speed of transport and methods of building, four hundred years later, in the hour of their decline, it is difficult to find that significant progress has been made in any of these things. To the end of their time, for instance, the Romans never succeeded in devising a set of harness for their beasts of burden that did not half-choke them.

Worse still, when in the middle period of the Empire slave-labour began to be less plentiful (for there were practically no external wars to produce new slaves and freedom by manumission was reducing the number of existing ones), recourse had to be made to recruiting for the defence of the frontiers those who lived outside them. Thus barbarians were, in effect, being invited in to taste the fruits of a higher civilisation which, in the end, even they must have realised, were theirs for the taking. It may be that it was not the lack of technical science in itself that cost the Romans their Empire in the West. But surely, pre-eminence in technical science even combined with a degree of moral decline, could have saved it. Be that as it may, the nations of the West are trusting that the proposition is true of our own day and age.

By their considerable powers of administration, Diocletian and Constantine can be said to have halted economic decline, but when they had passed from the scene, it again gathered momentum. To a greater or lesser extent, economic difficulties had been the lot of the Romans since the time when their Empire had reached the limits of expansion: now, aggravated by the heavy cost of repelling barbaric invasions, they were producing serious political effects, nowhere more clearly manifested than in Spain, which after the Franco-Suevian raid early in the second half of the third century enjoyed a long period of freedom from molestation from outside.

More and more, as world trade dwindled, the rich were abandoning the Spanish towns and were building themselves vast, self-sufficient estates (latifundia) out in the countryside where, incidentally, their transactions were less liable to supervision by Treasury officials. At least two of their vast country houses, complete with chapel, like eighteenth-century houses in England, have been discovered in recent excavations near Fraga and Badajoz. In them can be seen the prototypes of the medieval system: for they were staffed by large numbers of persons, who were content to accept virtual serfdom under the protection of a patron in exchange for a precarious existence as freemen in a State-run town. For local government in the towns was becoming increasingly rigid, as popular elections became a thing of the past because, with the elimination of the middle class, the first victims of the slump, there were no longer sufficient candidates of good quality to volunteer, and nominations to office were made by higher officials in the Emperor's private Civil Service.

In the wider world outside, after the death of Constantine, the question of whether to divide or not divide the Empire became the shuttlecock of successive Emperors. First a new bout of civil war divided it, Constantius (A.D. 353-361) united it. In 364 the brothers Valentinian and Valens undid it again. Theodosius (379-395) put it together again, and under the latter's two sons, although the legal figment of two halves comprising one whole Empire was maintained, in fact the breach proved permanent, if for no better reason than that the West—and Spain with it—collapsed finally under the assaults of the barbarian invaders.

It so happened that the final convulsion that brought Roman rule in Spain to an end occurred at a time when the Roman Emperors were again Spaniards or directly descended from Spaniards. Theodosius was a native of Cauca (Coca, north-west of Segovia) and was living in Spain with his Spanish wife on his estate between Valladolid and Segovia when he was called to the throne in an atmosphere of crisis. His predecessor, Valens, had fallen a victim to a serious Visigothic incursion at Adrianople. Theodosius thus made his mark early in his reign by restoring the situation in the Balkans and, a little later, by suppressing the pretensions of his fellow Spaniard, Maximus, won a brief period of peace for his harassed subjects. Among the many panegyrics from which not even the best of Emperors could escape, one delivered in the year A.D. 389 by a Gallic orator named Pacatus has survived. But it is so obviously a piece of fulsome court flattery that not even the references to Spain that it contained are worthy of repetition.

Unfortunately, harmony did not prevail for long between his two young sons, Arcadius and Honorius, when, on their father's death, they again divided the Empire, and in A.D. 402 Stilicho, Honorius's general in the West, was hard put to it to defeat at Pollentia in Liguria (A.D. 402) Alaric and his German followers, who had launched an unexpected attack upon Italy with the connivance, if not the active support, of the other brother. The price that he had to pay for this temporary success was the stripping of the Rhine of all its garrisons, thus opening the flood-gates to the Suevi and Vandals. Seven years later there was no Stilicho there to offer further resistance. In the autumn of A.D. 409 the Vandals, Alans and Suevi poured over the last barrier of the Pyrenees and, in the following year, Rome itself was sacked by the persistent and vengeful Alaric.

The Spanish provinces proved an easy prey for the three Teutonic tribes: indeed, Gerontius, the Emperor's military commander in the Peninsula, had got himself so heavily involved in a fresh round of Emperor-making, that the invasion for him represented cover against powerful personal rivals. But the situation was soon completely out of hand. Sweeping down the west side, the invaders were within two years in effective control of the whole country. An arrangement made in A.D. 411 between them and the Emperor of the truncated West, which referred to them as 'federati' could not conceal the end of Roman rule in Spain, and the arrival, shortly afterwards, of another Teutonic tribe, the Visigoths, to dispossess them merely underlined that fact. What did remain constant was the character of the Spanish people. The inhabitants of Galicia and of the Sierra Morena were not completely reconciled to their new masters until the time of Leovigildus, nearly one hundred and fifty years later.

CHAPTER IX

Public Buildings and Their Function

THERE is always a danger that a first visit to a Roman site may prove a disappointment, even for those who have spent some years of their life studying the language and reading the history. Too often, in Britain, at any rate, it means viewing foundations that have been unearthed from below ground-level, and few people have the necessary powers of imagination to make the realities of modern excavation match the greatness that, they are told, was Rome's. The possibility of disillusionment is less likely on the Continent, where massive Roman buildings have survived, a few of them in their entirety. On a first visit, the Pont du Gard, for instance, can have almost an emotional impact on many who have stood, tongue-tied, in embarrassment, only too conscious of their own shortcomings, when confronted with the excavations of the enthusiastic archaeologists at home. None the less, appreciation of the largest and most impressive Roman building is heightened if something is known of its background and of the reason why it was put there. So this chapter will be devoted to a description of the functions of those public buildings that have survived in Spain, in whole or in part, from the days of Rome.

But first, a brief word about the major contribution that the Romans made to the evolution of the art of building, a contribution that can be summed up in a single phrase—the rounded arch. The Greeks had been blessed with a superb sense of proportion and symmetry, and verticals, joined at the top by flat horizontals, had provided them with all the means that they required for expressing their genius. The rounded arch, there is reason to think, was brought to the Romans by the Etruscans, their neighbours immediately to the north of the Tiber, who, in the earliest days of the city's existence, supplied Rome with two unpopular kings. Whatever the origin of the arch, characteristically the Romans put it to good practical use: they incorporated it into the construction of the 'cloaca maxima', their first attempt at city sewage, and from this prosaic start it proceeded to permeate all Roman buildings as though it were its trade-mark, and to dominate the architecture of Western Europe for a thousand years, until the Moors introduced the Arabic arch into the south of Spain.

AQUEDUCTS

There could hardly be a better advertisement for the arch than the aqueduct, for which (so many did they build) the Romans might well be suspected of having had a weakness. But behind this apparent extravagance lay a sound reason, one that occurs, possibly on second thoughts only, to visitors from our own well-watered islands. By contrast, the climate of Southern Europe—of Spain above all—is so much more prone to drought that, if good springs of water are available, then, within reason, distance is no object to supplies being piped to where they are most needed.

The channel through which the water flowed had, of course, so to be engineered as to have a slight slope in the required direction: rarely, on its lengthy journey, is the water conveyed across the series of arches that we associate with the word 'aqueduct': only when the lie of the land made it inevitable was recourse made to this artificial means of conveying water. The channel itself was made of brick or stone, lined with cement, and provided at intervals with vent-holes: sometimes lead pipes were used inside the channel. The aqueduct started from some form of reservoir, and other reservoirs were made at stages along its course. At the end of its course the water was allowed to flow into a large chamber, from which it passed into three containers, the centre being lower than the other two and so receiving water only from the overflow of the other two: the two outer containers supplied private houses and the public baths, the centre one the public fountains and circus and amphitheatre: so, in times of water shortage, the less essential needs were the first to be cut. As a rule a handsome building enclosed this first dividing of the waters and was known as a 'castellum'; from the chief castellum the water was diverted to other smaller castella where the same principle of temporary storage was used as in the main one. 'Castella' that were wholly for private use were built at the joint expense of the families who used them, but all were under the general supervision of the public officers responsible for the water supplies (curatores aquarum).

These officers had a very considerable technical and supervising staff to help them, their chief objectives being the maintenance of the water channel in good repair and the prevention of fraudulent diversion of the water. One section of the staff was detailed to repairs of the channel, a second to the supervision of the 'castella', a third to the inspection and maintenance of the actual superstructure of an aqueduct and a fourth to that section of the water supplies that passed directly under city streets.

The finest aqueduct in Spain—and one which challenges the more famous Pont du Gard in the south of France, if only because it is still in working order—is at Segovia. Water is piped from springs in the Sierra de Fuenfria 10 miles to the south-east and, before spanning the valley in which the town lies, passes into the water tower called el Caseron. Then it runs across the aqueduct proper, almost exactly half a mile long, not altogether in a direct line; at about one-fifth of the distance from the south-east it inclines very slightly to the left, and again at the half-distance more definitely to the right. The double row of arches, one hundred and twenty-eight in all, are built of white, Aberdeen-like granite, cut and squared by masons and put together without the aid of cement. At its highest point over the Plaza de Azoguejo it is just over 90 feet high: on the top of the four lower arches, just above the streets, is an additional section of stonework rectangular in shape, obviously intended to carry the date of construction, which is now missing. It is thought, however, to date from the time of Augustus (died A.D. 14), and it is known that a section of it was restored in 1483.

BATHS

The public baths, it will be noticed, were the only public institutions to share priority of water supply with private needs, a measure of the importance that the Romans attached to this particular amenity. They were usually built in the suburbs, and in the more important cities there were several. Relics of at least two have been discovered in Merida, for instance. The reason for them, in the first place, from the earliest days of the Republic, was the normal one of cleanliness, and originally they were provided for the many people who were not able to install such amenities inside their own homes. Later, under the Empire, public baths assumed the proportions of major public works, but at all times the price of admission was set well within the means of the poorest citizen; women were not, in general, encouraged to participate, and if they did they were charged a higher fee for the privilege; but separate accommodation was available and it is likely that the higher charge was caused by the fact that fewer people used it. Mixed bathing did occur, but it was never accepted as respectable and both Hadrian and Marcus Aurelius took steps to stop it, in the second century A.D.

The popular hour for bathing was in the afternoon as a preliminary to the main meal of the day; the process was more akin to our Turkish bath than to our normal habit of having a 'dip'. First there was the 'apodyterium', where all clothing was removed and committed to the charge of slaves, who were not always above a little petty larceny, we are told. Then there was the 'frigidarium' (which explains itself) for those who wanted a cold bath; however, if this were by-passed, the customer proceeded to sit in the 'tepidarium', which was heated by a moderately warm air, where he was anointed by unguents that were stored in a separate room. Next he entered the 'caldarium', the high temperature of which was maintained by a hypocaust beneath the floor: a few more elaborate baths provided a sweating room of even higher temperature, known as a 'laconicum', a round room with a domed ceiling. After perspiration, the bather was scraped down with a bone or metal scraper, the edge of which was softened with oil, before returning to the tepidarium to cool off. Finally, his clothes were brought back to him, he put them on and left for the street.

Put baldly like this, it may not sound a very attractive proposition. But in point of fact it was highly popular at all stages of Rome's history and was indulged in by every level of society, including the Emperor himself, and was invested with something of the 'club' atmosphere. From the time of Augustus public baths were expanded into something not far removed from community centres for young men, on the lines of the Greek gymnasium. In them, athletics could be practised and there were cool, columnated halls to act as common rooms for discussion, or idle talk, or for lectures by philosophers or recitations by poets. Remnants of upwards of a score of public baths of one sort or another have been unearthed in Spain, but this must be but a small percentage of those that once existed in what was, after all, one of the most prosperous parts of the Roman Empire.

THEATRES

Theatres, on the other hand, which, where possible, were built on to and out of the side of a hill, were less easily obliterated by the passage of time, if only because, very often, they occupied sites that no one in the succeeding centuries ever wanted to use again. Primarily, Roman theatres were Greek theatres, with slight modifications, and were, in the open air, exposed to the elements: where temporary cover was improvised for audience or performers, it was to protect them from the heat of the sun.

A theatre was built almost exactly in the shape of a half-circle whose two ends are joined by the line of the diameter represented by the straight edge of the front of the stage. The stage, raised an appreciable distance above the level of the ground immediately confronting it, was 20 to 25 feet broad, and was backed by a traditional and permanent set-piece representing the façade of a palace with a colonnade of pillars in front and the actors' quarters behind. Along the entire front of the stage and immediately at the foot of it ran a trench, perhaps 2 feet wide and 6 or more feet deep, in which masonry had been so built as to leave sockets into which square wooden pillars could be lowered: these pillars were the substructure that supported the curtain in front of the stage, the lowering of which was a signal for the start of the performance. The half-circle facing the stage was bowl-shaped and was occupied by rows of stone seats that ran parallel with the outer rim, each row the same degree lower than the one above it until the shortest row was on ground level, and so near the elevated stage as to make it unprofitable to construct more seats.

Consequently, between the front, arc-shaped row of seats and the centre of the front of the stage was a flat piece of unoccupied ground still known by its Greek title, the orchestra, and in this lay the main difference between the Roman theatre and the original Greek model. The Greek theatre occupied slightly more of a full circle than the Roman version did, and so the orchestra space was correspondingly larger, and in the centre of it, reminding the audience of the theatre's religious origin, stood an altar to Dionysus, around which were gathered the chorus who played so prominent a part in the original Greek tragedies.

Viewed from the stage, the auditorium or 'cavea', as it was called, had all the orderliness and neatness of the best terracing in our modern football grounds, having stairways that radiated symmetrically outwards giving access to the row of seats, and at least one level gangway allowing free movement between stairways on a horizontal plane: there was often such a gangway behind the fifteenth row, because by a law of 76 B.C. the first fifteen rows of a theatre were reserved for those of the business community who, on the basis of property ownership and wealth, were officially qualified as 'equites' or knights. In the provinces, visitors or residents who were of senatorial rank were accommodated on special seats set out in front.

The Romans showed admirable ingenuity in providing the necessary artificial banking on which to lay the stone seating. Where there was a natural site near a town, they were swift to take advantage of it, and where there were imperfections in the level of the hillside, instead of scooping away the ground to get a smooth base, they preferred to build up the hollows by the erection of shallow arches; or, very likely, there was a combination of both methods, because, whereas such arches as were made are visible, there is no evidence of mere transference of soil and stones.

But few towns were fortunate enough to have natural theatres on their doorstep. On the other hand, sufficient mound was usually available to support, or to be adapted to support, a considerable number of rows of seats: the remaining rows above were laid upon a cleverly devised series of vaulted arches, the roofs of which sloped downwards as their width tapered inwards. In the case of the larger theatres the height of the arch that supported the highest row of seats was such that recourse was had to the double layer of arches, as was common practice in aqueducts. At regular intervals and at a fixed height in the auditorium half an arch was left open and steps led down from it, providing exits (vomitoria) for the audience. The main entrances were two in number, leading in by a vaulted passage, one on each side, parallel to and adjoining the front of the stage. Above the entrance on the left of the audience was a 'tribunal' or special 'box' reserved, as in the modern bull-ring, for the person of honour who presided over the performance.

The performances given were comedies, tragedies and farces and, most popular of all, mimes, a form of low comedy with vulgar characters speaking in vulgar language, the counterpart of the lowest form of music-hall sketch, with no restraint from the Lord Chamberlain. With the advance of education, under the Emperors, there developed the pantomime, in which a whole story was represented by the movements and gestures of a single dancer, who appeared successively in various characters, to the accompaniment of music sung by a chorus: the themes represented were mainly love stories and a number of Ovid's poems were adapted to this medium. Successful 'pantomimi' were fêted, but in general actors did not come from the higher levels of society.

The best specimen of a Roman theatre in Spain is to be found in Merida: in detail it differs from the general description given above because Roman Spain in some respects is more akin to Roman Africa than to Roman Gaul. Visitors to Merida should not expect the amount of restoration that has been done in France at Orange, or even at Arles. Indeed, before 1910 there would have been very little in the way of a theatre to see in Merida. For it was in that year that work was started on the excavation of it.

The auditorium is divided into three sections: the first three rows were obviously intended for senators and distinguished visitors: behind these is a paved gangway, above which rise twenty more rows, topped by a second gangway: finally, to complete the accommodation, a further ten rows for the rank and file. Originally the front three rows were dressed with marble, the rest with stone: presumably the occupants provided their own cushions. The top range of seats has six evenly spaced 'vomitoria', apertures that lead directly downwards to the outside: the gangway immediately below the top range has five exits also leading directly back to the outside. In contrast, however, evenly spaced about two-thirds of the way up the centre block of seats, are six more exits that give on to an underground gallery, which, following the line of the rows built on top of it, has two exits, one at each end, near the main entrance. In the centre of the bottom row of the centre block was a special oblong platform that was reserved for the imperial 'legatus' who was governor of the province. It is estimated that the theatre would hold 5,500 persons.

The 'orchestra' still retains its marble paving: the stage ('pulpitum') is some 65 yards long by 8 yards wide: in front are twelve holes—not a trench—9 feet deep, for the woodwork connected with the stage curtain. The front elevation of the stage was dressed with marble. The traditional set-piece of the palace with

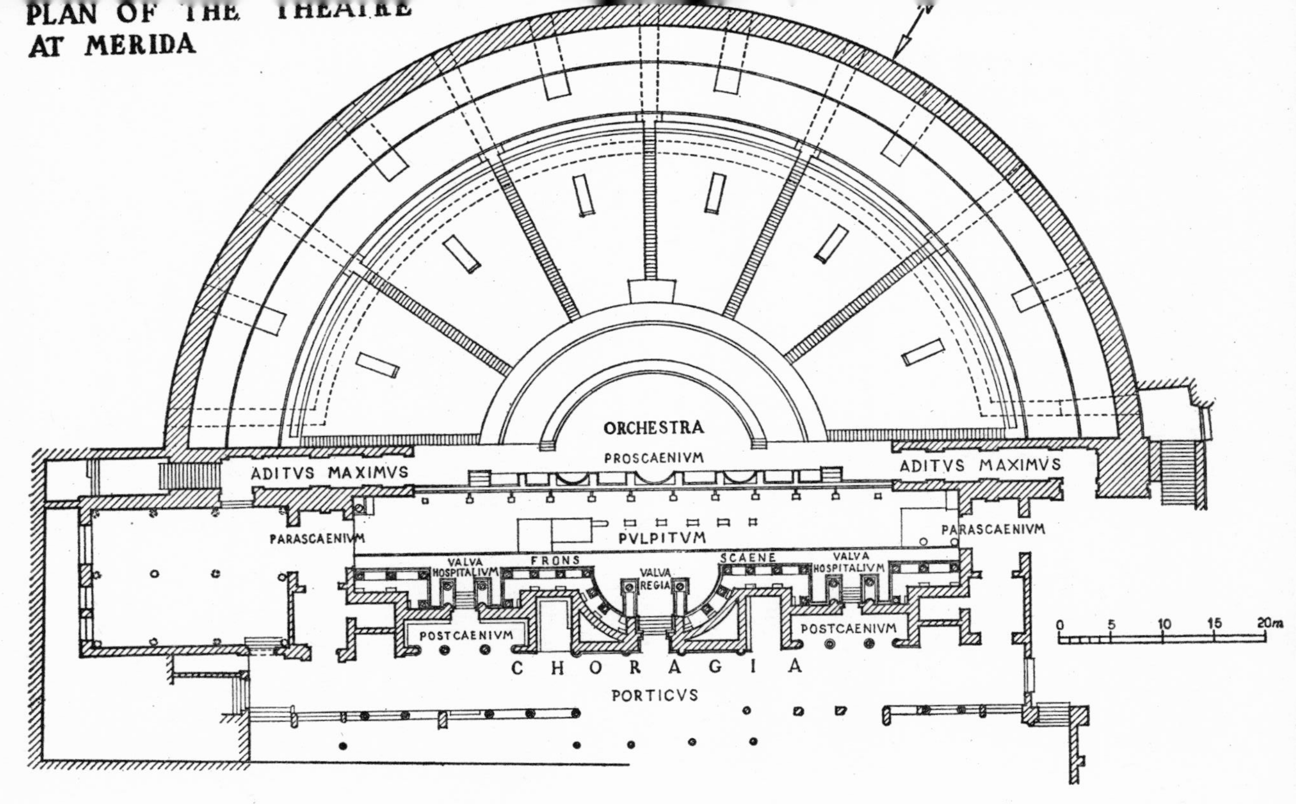
PLAN OF THE THEATRE
AT MERIDA
ORCHESTRA
PROSCAENIVM
ADITVS MAXIMVS
ADITVS MAXIMVS
PARASCAENIVM
PARASCAENIVM
PVLPITVM
FRONS
SCAENE
VALVA HOSPITALIVM
VALVA HOSPITALIVM
VALVA REGIA
POSTCAENIVM
POSTCAENIVM
C H O R A G I A
PORTICVS
0
5
10
15
20m

the three doors had been treated with a richness unusual in a provincial theatre: along the full length of its façade ran a double colonnade of Corinthian pillars, the blue shafts of which contrasted with the white of capital and base. A section of this colonnade has been reconstructed *in situ* and some of the statues that adorned it have also been put back. The statues represented Ceres, Pluto, Proserpine, Bacchus, Venus, three emperors —probably Augustus, Trajan and Hadrian—and two other unidentifiable persons wearing togas. Those not replaced are to be seen in the local museum. Backstage were the actors' quarters, and the rear of the building was completed by an extensive and stylish portico.

The date of the theatre is beyond doubt. Over the doorways of the two main vaulted entrances that lead from the side directly into the orchestra is inscribed the name of Marcus Agrippa and the reference to the number of times that he has been consul fixes the year as 18 B.C. The fact that Merida was equipped with a theatre of these dimensions within seven years of the founding of the town itself is indicative of the importance that the Romans attached to the provision of this amenity. Fragments of an inscription that were found suggest that the colonnade was erected in the reign of Hadrian (A.D. 117-137), and the signatures of Greek workmen on some of the capitals reinforce the suggestion: for Hadrian was a great admirer of Greek workmanship. There is also some slight evidence of restoration work undertaken in the time of Constantine early in the fourth century.

AMPHITHEATRES

By its derivation, the word 'amphitheatre' means double theatre and, if we are to believe the elder

Pliny, the prototype was just that. According to him, Caius Curio, a partisan of Julius Caesar, constructed two wooden theatres that stood on revolving bases, which, when turned straight edge to straight edge, formed an amphitheatre for the exhibition of gladiators or wild beasts. This scarcely credible account, given by Pliny more than a century after the alleged event, is probably no more than an apocryphal story to illustrate the meaning of the word 'amphitheatre': for, granted that the whole is an ellipse and not a circle, an amphitheatre is most readily described as two theatres set facing one another, without their stages.

The centre thus left free, elliptical in shape, was called the 'arena' because, for the various bloody performances that were given on it, the floor was covered with a generous amount of sand. There were usually three main entrances leading into the arena: two facing each other diametrically opposite at the narrow ends of the ellipse, and one halfway down one of the two longer sides. At least two of the entrances had platforms built over them, adjacent to the arena, seats of especial honour to be occupied respectively by the presiding magistrate and the person at whose expense the show was being given. In many amphitheatres, underneath a nearby section of the audience there was a rest-room, to which the person of honour could withdraw for refreshment during the long hours of the performance.

Round the edge of the arena stood a wall (podium) faced with marble, 8 or 9 feet high, topped by railings, for the safety of the spectators: on the podium sat the other magistrates and senators. Behind, rising from above a gangway, were the rest of the seats, the business class (equites) first and the rank and file higher still. The construction of the auditorium was on the same general lines as those given above for the theatre, though there are, of course, differences of detail, both between amphitheatre and theatre and between one amphitheatre and another. Some were built on entirely flat ground, when the whole of the seating is set upon arcades: others had one side of the bowl on a natural hillside and the other side raised on arcades: a few were constructed with help from two hills, as at Italica, but none could dispense with artificial means of elevation altogether.

The larger amphitheatres appear to have been equipped with subterranean galleries beneath the arena from their earliest days, which were the first of the Empire under Augustus. The one at Merida, built as early as 8 B.C., is so equipped and there is nothing about the method of construction of the galleries to lead one to suspect that they were later additions. Here a large rectangle in the centre of the arena with two smaller ones projecting from it, one on each side, down the line of the longer axis of the ellipse, had subterranean chambers or passages beneath, and would be boarded over and, along with the rest of the arena, covered with sand. At Italica (Santiponce) the underground section occupies about the same proportion of the arena and is much the same shape.

On the other hand, Puteoli, in Italy, had no fewer than forty-six trap-doors in the arena, whilst in the Colosseum itself the whole floor space was occupied by underground rooms and passages. But, extensive or restricted, they served the same purpose: into some were removed the dead or dying of the performers, be they men or beasts: from others the wild animals were launched into the arena from cages, which were lifted up to ground-level by hoist and pulley worked from below by slaves.

The gladiators were of two types, either slaves, condemned criminals and the like, or free men from all grades of society and, occasionally, even women, who learned their technical skill from trainers (lanistae). Slave gladiators were either owned by 'lanistae' or by men of wealth who would hire 'lanistae' to train them. In the arena the fights were fought with varying weapons and the combats were 'Thracian' or 'Gallic' to the audience according to the type of weapon used, much in the same way as the audience at a fencing match today recognises instantly the difference between foil and sabre. Other bouts were fought from chariots, and one of the commonest forms of duel was that between a man armed with a sword (secutor) and another armed with net and trident (retiarius). But whatever the type of combat, when one of the pair was at the mercy of his opponent, the crowd indicated by a gesture of the thumb whether they wished him to be dispatched or not.

Fights between animals or between man and beast came under the general title of 'venatio' (hunting). A man might be matched against a lion, a tiger, a bull or a bear, or virtually any animal might be pitted against any other, e.g. rhinoceros *versus* bull. Alternatively, tamed beasts were exhibited and put through their tricks: elephants danced, leopards were yoked, stags and bears were bridled.

The analogy between one of the styles of combat mentioned in the last paragraph and the bull-fight of modern Spain is easy to see and, perhaps, justifies a brief digression to trace the connection between the two. Combats between man and bull were not conjured up by the Romans: for they were popular in Campania before they became so in Rome, and in Thessaly in Greece. As early as the time of the Trojan War there were contests between bull and man, although they are described more as bull-baitings than bull-fights, on the style of the 'novilladas' so common in Spain today, when young bulls are released into the stockaded plaza of a town (e.g. in Pamplona at the festival of San Firmin in July) and the young men of the district test their skill and strength in unarmed combat with them. The cult of the legend of the bull as the enemy of man was widespread all round the Mediterranean, emanating, possibly, from the story of the Minotaur in Crete.

However, it was the Moors who introduced the bull-fight more or less in the form that we know today, when they invaded the south of Spain from North Africa during the seventh century A.D. Under their régime, bull-fights were regularly staged in the half-ruined amphitheatres of Merida, Cordoba, Toledo and Tarragona. After their expulsion early in the fifteenth century bull-fights became a form of aristocratic sport; even the great Charles V took part. The Moorish style of combat was still retained: that is to say the man fought from horseback and the bull was finally killed by a thrust of a lance: it was not until the beginning of the eighteenth century that the matador was introduced on foot to administer the *coup de grâce* with his sword. With the advent of professionalism have come the many bull-rings throughout Spain, none of which is much more than a hundred years old.

CIRCUSES

An especial effort of the imagination is required to visualise the circuses of Roman Spain in full use, because only vestiges of some remain and only literary evidence for one or two others, e.g. Cadiz. But there are visible remains at Tarragona, Calahorra (beyond Saragossa up the Ebro valley), Saguntum, Toledo and Merida, and considerable work has been done on this last. In addition, two fine mosaics, representing a circus in use, have been found in Gerona and Barcelona and are kept in the museum of the latter city.

Horseracing was the sport even of Roman kings before the foundation of the Republic in 509 B.C. For it was Tarquinius Priscus who built the first Roman circus, albeit most of it in wood. But it was not until the last days of the Republic and the early days of the Empire that the use of them for horse- and chariot-racing became widespread. By the nature of their function, their shape remained fundamentally the same, of oblong form with one end almost straight and the other completed in a half-circle.

The overall length of a circus was three or four times the full width of it. In the centre of the straight end was an entrance: on either side of it, six enclosures (carceres) long enough for each to contain a chariot and team, were so set as to deliver the competitors towards the right side of the circus floor: for races were always run anticlockwise. Down the centre, inclining slightly from left to right to supply the maximum of space after the turn, ran the 'spina', a narrow wall some 4 feet high, around which the laps of the race were run. At each end of the 'spina' stood a 'meta', a bronze post, grazed by the chariot wheels on the turn. The winning post was marked by a white line on the floor, halfway down one side of the 'spina', opposite the place where the judges sat. On the 'spina' itself stood six posts supporting six egg-shaped balls, one of which was removed at the end of each completed lap. Otherwise the 'spina' was adorned by an obelisk or statue of honour in the centre, but not of such proportions as seriously to impede the view of the spectators. In the centre of the semicircular end was the gate out of which the winner departed after a triumphal parade of the course.

The seating arrangements were in the usual style of theatre and amphitheatre, both in the social grading and in construction, with the reservation, in respect of the latter, that there was some use of wood for the top seats, because it must be remembered that a circus covered a good deal of ground: that at Merida, for instance, measuring 470 by 124 yards. The president of the meeting had a traditional seat of honour, in a 'box' built over the 'carceres' or starting gate.

Chariot-racing in particular was a dangerous business: there were separate races for two-horse teams and for four-horse teams. The driver traditionally drove with the reins looped round his waist, and this added considerably to his peril in any of the frequent smashes that occurred, although he carried a knife upon his person with which to extricate himself. There was heavy betting on the results and successful drivers could win big money in a short time. As for the horses, Spain is listed with Thessaly, Sicily and North Africa as their source.

Finally, it was not uncommon for mock sea battles to be staged in an amphitheatre or a circus, although it is difficult to see how this could be done in those amphitheatres equipped with underground premises. A circus would presumably not present the same difficulty. There is evidence at Merida to suggest that water could be piped from a nearby aqueduct to flood the circus: how often that amount of water could be spared, in Estremadura of all districts, is another question.

TEMPLES

Here again the Roman model was an adaptation of the Greek prototype, as represented by the familiar Parthenon at Athens. The base on which the pillars stood was raised considerably and access to it was by a flight of steps at the front end: the inner core of the temple, the 'cella', the enclosed building containing the altar, often with no other illumination than that provided by the opened door, was withdrawn from the centre of the columns towards that half of the base remote from the steps. Beyond this basic layout there were variations of detail that were acknowledged by various titles. Where the side walls of the cella projected towards the steps—terminating, as likely as not, in a pilaster—then such a temple was known as 'in antis'. Other titles depended on the arrangement of the pillars. Temples with a line of pillars on the top of the steps were 'prostyle', and the number of such pillars was recorded in Greek derivatives, viz. tetrastyle (4), hexastyle (6), etc. A temple having columns surrounding the entire building was 'peripteral'; when, under this arrangement, the side columns were engaged in the wall of the 'cella' instead of standing clear, it was termed 'pseudo-peripteral'. In practice, the Romans liked to have twice as many inter-columnar spaces down the side of the temple as there were in front of it. So if there were six or eight columns on the front, there were eleven or fifteen down each side.

A final word of technical explanation for the various types of columns. They are far more readily distinguishable by their capitals than by their bases, which in all four orders are, to the uninitiated, distressingly alike. The Doric pillar is usually fluted and at the top of the capital had a plain unadorned, rectangular slab: the series of groups of three grooves (triglyphs) along the frieze above is an indispensable adjunct of the Doric style. An Ionic pillar is more slender and its capital easily recognised by the volutes that project one from each side. The Corinthian style is the commonest: here the capital is much deeper than in the other two and is decorated by bold carving of acanthus leaves, reminiscent, in general, of the Early English among Gothic styles. To the above three versions of the original Greek styles, passing by the same name, Rome added two others, neither, however, betraying much originality. First, a so-called Composite order, a mixture of Corinthian and Ionic capitals: second, the Tuscan order, best explained as the Doric without the attendant triglyphs.

Temples have not found it easy to survive, if only because few things are so out of date as a discarded religion or few people so destructive as the converted fanatic, and, on a more practical level, they were usually built in the centre of towns and commanded little sympathy when the time came for development to take place. In the more obvious show-places, such as Rome or Athens, or Nimes, temples have survived in various stages of completeness as the result of conscious efforts at preservation or restoration. Spain is conspicuous for no such efforts. But even so there are remains of sufficient temples, dedicatory altars, etc., in Spain to warrant some consideration of the history of religion in the Peninsula of which these stones are the surviving symbols.

Not unnaturally, the religious beliefs of the Iberians have been overlaid by those of their Roman conquerors almost to the point of obliteration. Inscriptions to local deities, whose names are entirely barbarous save that the words are Latinised, have been found fairly frequently in Lusitania, Galicia and Asturias (e.g. Endovelicus, Bormanicus, Tongoenabiagus and Durbedicus) and a few in the district of Clunia and Saragossa in the Ebro valley: rarely round Cartagena, and never round Tarragona or in the province of Baetica. These local deities are thought to have been streams and springs, deified in the simple, direct way of a primitive people.

Religion had had an equally simple beginning for the Romans—in the home: Vesta, the goddess of the hearth: the Penates, the guardians of the larder: the Lares, who watched over their fields: Janus, the door god who connected the family with the outside world, and vice versa: the 'genius', the life-spirit of each generation of the family. In the wider world outside were Jupiter, Juno, Mars and the rest, who were never thought of as possessed of human form, as were Greek gods by the Greeks.

From the religion of the home was developed a State religion, with a fixed calendar and code of ritual and a list of appropriate sacrifices. The State was interested only to secure the goodwill of the gods and, since religion was in no sense a way of life, there was no need for a priestly order other than a committee of fifteen, under a chief pontiff (pontifex maximus), to concern itself with the legal side of religion: there were other committees of priests to supervise divination, the taking of auspices and the ritual of peace-making, and of the declaration of war.

This rigid and negative form of religion was put to the test and proved inadequate during the recurrent crises of the Second Punic War. In their despair after the battle of Cannae, the Romans even had recourse to human sacrifice and, in 205 B.C., the Senate officially authorised the introduction of the worship of the Earth Goddess Cybele from Asia Minor, and by 191 B.C. she had a temple of her own on the Palatine. This cult and that of Dionysus (Bacchus), which followed later, had strong elements of mysticism which, while alien to the original Roman character, did provide a much-needed emotional outlet.

An integral part of Augustus's campaign for the revival of the ancient Roman virtues was a recall to the ancient Roman gods, whose status had been seriously impaired not only by the importations from the East, but by the repeated outbursts of civil war that marked the last century B.C. up to the foundation of the Empire. As a practical measure towards this end, eighty-two temples dedicated to the ancient gods were restored and in 23 B.C. a small new temple was built on the Capitol in Rome, dedicated to Jupiter the Thunderer, in gratitude for the safe return of the Emperor from the perils of the Cantabrian War in Spain. The motive of gratitude was a reflection of a movement started six years earlier in the East, where ruler-cult had always been a regular feature of its early history. The Bithynians were given permission to dedicate a temple jointly to Rome and Augustus at Nicaea; the Greeks followed suit at Pergamum and the idea spread to the West, with perhaps, some little encouragement from official sources; for the benefits that were to be reaped by way of unification, from the successful transplanting of such a cult, were obvious: in 12 B.C. an altar, so dedicated, was erected at Lyons by the tribes of Gaul.

But in Spain the introduction of the cult was much delayed: a temple to Augustus, now deified after his death, was built at Tarragona shortly after A.D. 14, but it was at least another forty years before the cult was widely accepted throughout Lusitania and Baetica: only for Augustus, whose merits were widely recognised, was it reinforced by any sincerity of feeling and, although it was maintained long after his time, for later emperors it had little more religious significance than the ceremony of saluting the flag.

Owing to the vast ramifications of her many-sided trade, despite her comparative remoteness in the west, Spain was never likely to be omitted in any westward spread of Eastern religions. No religion, however, not even the religion of Rome, should be considered as sweeping the entire Peninsula; in general a region was only capable of assimilating new ideas in so far as it was already romanised, and in the virtually complete absence of anything that could vaguely be described as mission work, large sections of the west and north of the country must, at heart, have remained loyal to the beliefs of their Iberian ancestors. A pagan altar stone has been found 20 kms. west of Santander, dedicated to an unknown god, Erudinus, and bearing the precise date of August 23rd, A.D. 399. Even in the rest of the country new religions tended to exist in pockets rather than to have universal application.

New ideas in the first century A.D. were synonymous with the cults of Isis and Mithras which gained popularity in the West at that time. Isis came from Egypt: she was the all-powerful queen of heaven and earth, of life and death, who appealed strongly to the emotions by the annual festival of remembrance for the death of her consort, Osiris. The cult of Mithras, on the other hand, having been directly imported from Persia by troops who had served there, was much more a religion for men. Above all, he was the champion of light against the powers of darkness: as St. George slew the dragon, so he had slain the bull. Hence ritual bull slaying, involving blood baptism for initiates, was part of his cult.

But the surest testimony to the diversity of gods is supplied by the archaeological finds of inscribed votive altars or altar-stones. These often take the form of a marble monolith, square or rectangular, occasionally cylindrical, not more than a yard high: the dedicatory inscription is usually in a rectangular inset on the front, sometimes with the carving of a garland or of a sacred vessel on the sides or rear: in general, they were erected inside the sacred enclosure of a temple by people who had promised under certain conditions to do so, or were grateful for some piece of good fortune. It will be noticed that they do not all honour gods as persons but that some of them do honour to abstractions (such as Concord or Victory), so preserving the earliest precedents of Roman family religion.

The Archaeological Museum at Tarragona has an altar dedicated to the tutelary spirit (genius) of the province by a slave called Baba in gratitude for having completed the building of a temple without accident: a second in fulfilment of a vow to Jupiter by Afrania

Tertuliana: and a third, with the same dedication as the first by L. Municius Aprontanus, one of the two chief magistrates of a town.

From among the many in the National Archaeological Museum in Madrid the following are quoted, with their place of origin in brackets: to Apollo (Jaen); to Bacchus (Arjona); to Concordia Augusta (Mancha Real); to Cybele (Merida) by Valeria Avita to commemorate her initiation; to Diana (Almonacid, in the province of Leon); to Hercules (Alcala de Henares); to Minerva (Clunia, Coruña del Conde); to the Nymphs of a stream (Ledesma in the province of Leon); to Safety (Cartagena); to victorious Venus (Merida); to Victory (Italica). In the Casa de Pilatos at Seville is the base of a statue of Isis that was found at Guadix: it is the gift of a woman, one Fabia Fabrana, and on its sides, carved in relief, are the white stork and the bull that were associated with the cult in Egypt. Altars from what must have been a temple of Mithras were found in Merida: on the sides, carved in relief, are instruments of sacrifice executed in a style that suggests the second century A.D. Finally, two votive altars given in gratitude for cures effected by medicinal waters, at Montemayor (near Caceres) by various Romans and at Alange near Badajoz by the parents of a young boy who there recovered his health.

Christianity, therefore, came as just another religion—but with a difference. First, it was actively and widely preached by the apostles; secondly, it was opposed to all other religions. Its followers were persecuted from time to time, not because it was in itself a subversive religion, but because it was so intolerant of other beliefs. There was sufficient of a religious act associated with emperor-worship to make the Christian reject it and he was, therefore, persecuted on political grounds as a disloyal citizen. Incidentally, striking proof of the power of the belief in the other gods was provided by the fact that the early Christians acknowledged their existence, but thought that they were the creations of the powers of darkness.

It is reasonable to conjecture that Christianity was first heard of in Spain as early as the apostolic period in the first century. The claim has indeed been made that Spain was evangelised by St. James the Great and his journey along the north of Spain to Santiago de Compostela is offered as evidence. But not only is the story paralleled by similarly misleading stories about other contemporary saints in Provence, but it also ignores the fact that St. James was martyred in Jerusalem before the Apostles were dispersed.

An entry in the Martyrology of Adon, who wrote at Vienne in the ninth century, to the effect that St. Peter sent seven bishops into Spain is likewise suspect, since it is confirmed in no other Martyrology. Yet the head of this mission is said to have founded the church of the 'Civitas Accitana' (Guadix east of Granada) and when about the year A.D. 300 a council, famous in the religious history of Spain, was held at nearby Illiberis (Elvira, which has never been actually located, but can scarcely be distinguishable from Granada), the Bishop of Acci presided over it, possibly, but unhappily not conclusively, because his was recognised as the mother church of Spain. The places represented by the other bishops attending the conference are significant as showing how far Christianity had spread, but, with the possible exception of Galicia, there are no surprises. There was, therefore, a bishop from Galicia, two from the province of Tarragona, three from Lusitania and twenty-one from Baetica, and eight from the province of Cartagena.

Before this, the only evidence relating to the church in Spain in the third century concerns itself solely with persecutions: under the persecutions of Decius (A.D. 244-249) the Bishops of Leon-cum-Astorga and of Merida proved disloyal to their faith. By way of contrast, Fructuosus, the Bishop of Saragossa, was martyred along with his deacons in the reign of Valerian (A.D. 253-260), and under Diocletian (A.D. 284-305) Christian blood was shed in Seville, Cordoba, Calahorra, Italica, Barcelona and Gerona, and many of the records of the early church were destroyed. Also martyred in this, the last persecution the Christians had to suffer from Rome, were Felix at Gerona, Cucufas at Barcelona, Aciselus and Zoellus at Cordoba and Eulalia at Merida.

A word of caution is here necessary on the subject of bishops in this context: their position should not be equated with that of a modern bishop, with a palace and a diocese staffed with priests. In the early days of the Church it is almost true to say that there were bishops before there were priests. When quite a small number of conversions had been made in a community, a bishop was put in charge, with deacons to help with the liturgy and with the work devoted to the poor. In Rome itself Christian churches are known to have been built before the fourth century, but in the provinces the centre of worship was much more makeshift.

During the First World War there was excavated in Merida the remains of a private Roman house that had been converted into a church, and at the same time into a residence for the bishop and his staff. Known today as the Casa-Basilica Romana, it lies very close to the west end of the rear premises of the Roman theatre. A doorway led into the traditional atrium (or patio) of a good-class Roman house. The equally traditional 'impluvium' for gathering of rain-water lies, not in the centre of the patio, but in the north-east angle, a position that strongly suggests that, possibly at the time of adaptation, the patio was enlarged: however, the patio, as at present revealed, was surrounded by columns that supported the roof, and the bases of these are still *in situ*. The roofed gallery that ran round the outer side of these columns gave access to the surrounding rooms. The rooms that were used for ceremonial and worship are the two at the eastern end of the patio. Both are rectangular and each has an apse built out at the far end, and it is interesting to note that each apse had three windows in the manner of later medieval churches. The larger room, on the right, was used as a place of worship: it has a pavement of mosaic and on the walls, painted figures, unfortunately incomplete, clothed in purple garments. A door leads directly into the smaller room on the left, which served as a baptistry: there were remains of an open bath in the floor, complete with channel for draining and in the walls, three curved recesses where the clothes of initiates were left during the ceremony of total immersion. Some form of Venetian blinds made of alabaster provided the necessary privacy.

As for the rest, under the conversion from house to church, the atrium or patio served the purpose of the narthex, which is so commonly found at the west end of many cathedrals: the most important of the rooms on the left of the patio still retained some traces of painting on its walls, and must have been the triclinium, where the so-called 'love feasts' of early Christianity, half-social, half-ritual, were prepared for the small congregation. The other rooms were occupied by the bishop and his staff of deacons.

These dispositions are confirmed by literary evidence. A certain deacon of Merida, called Paul, who lived in the seventh century, wrote that the original Christian church of Merida had two separate dedications, one of which was to St. John the Baptist, and that they were both under one roof and that a bishop in his room could hear voices from either sanctuary. Little doubt, therefore, that in this discovery, unique in Western Europe, there has been found a Christian church that, during the recurrent persecutions of the third century, was content to pass for a suburban house and was openly adapted for its purpose in the fourth century when Christianity was adopted as the religion of the state at the death of Constantine.

FORA

Finally, a brief explanation of the layout of the typical Roman provincial town: in Spain, in particular, where Romanisation proceeded at such a pace under Caesar and Augustus, there are many instances of towns built to this pattern. First of all a rectangular piece of land is defended by a wall. Two main streets bisect the rectangle, with no great mathematical precision, one linking the centres of the longer sides, the other the centres of the shorter. Where the two crossed each other was the forum, which was itself rectangular in shape, the shorter sides being two-thirds the length of the longer sides, according to the canons of Vitruvius, who was Augustus's expert on town planning. Around the forum stood a portico and behind the portico stood shops and such public buildings as a temple, a basilica, a curia, a granary or even a prison. Only two of these call for any further explanation: the curia was the council chamber where the local magistrates (duumviri) and their advisory committee held their deliberations. The basilica was a larger building, a public hall with at least a dual function: it served as a court of justice and as a place of business, a local stock exchange or bourse. It was an oblong building consisting of a central nave lit by clerestory windows, and two, lower, side aisles, each separated from the centre by a single row of columns. A distinctive feature was the semicircular vaulted apse at one end of the central nave, under which was placed a raised platform for the presiding officer of justice. When Christianity was adopted as the religion of the State, it was common practice to convert a basilica into a church, thus initiating that particular style of church construction.

CHAPTER X

Tarraconensis

IT is appropriate that any review of Roman monuments should start with Ampurias, on the southern edge of the Bay of Rosas near the little fishing port of La Escala, 24 kms. to the south-east of Figueras: for it was here that the Romans first landed in Spain under Cnaeus Scipio in 218 B.C. The ruins lie above the road, overlooking the bay where the original landing was made. The Roman town was built to the west of the Greek settlement that preceded it, and the line of the walls is still traceable, forming a rectangle, measuring 800 yards from north to south and 300 yards from east to west.

These are the outlines of the town founded by Julius Caesar in 45 B.C. Recent excavations have revealed an older wall of cyclopean type on which the Roman wall was built. The south gate survived, revealing an arch built of dressed stone. In the centre of the town on each side of the main street that leads in from this gate are the remnants of pillars, bases and capitals that marked the site of the forum. There have also been discovered the sites of the columns of a temple of unknown dedication; the platform has a double set of steps leading on to it, divided by what appears to have been a platform or rostrum: on the platform itself it is possible to trace the walls of the cella. At least one Roman house has been laid bare, the rooms leading off typically from a tetrastyle patio.

Other discoveries are the base of a large funeral tower, a form of mausoleum, introduced by the Phoenicians, and of an underground water cistern, oblong in shape, some 22 yards long, with a series of arches down the centre to provide support for the vaulted roof that once covered it. Latest reports speak of definite signs of an amphitheatre, but details are not yet available. At the western end of the Greek city stands a small museum where some of the local finds are housed: it contains some attractive model reproductions of buildings.

Apart from some items from the Roman city of Ampurias which are to be found in its museum, Gerona itself has nothing to recall its history under the Romans, when it was the see of one of the earliest Christian bishops. But outside the city, on the plain, are three funeral towers of Roman origin: one at Vilablareix to the south-west has a base with a moulding and the main shaft above: base and shaft have each got little arched recesses, lined with brick for the reception, presumably, of cinerary urns. A similar tower stands at Acuaviva, a few kms. further out. The third stands 2 kms. east of the Costa Brava resort of Lloret de Mar, which the Romans knew as Loryma. It has a base about 9 feet square and two upper sections, the higher of which is hollow, enclosing a small chamber some 3 feet 8 inches by 5 feet. There is also a recess at the top of the base for an urn. None of these towers has retained any inscriptions to reveal the identity of the persons for whom they were erected.

Nearby Tossa has the remains of a Roman villa to add to its list of charms. The attractions of the whole

Costa Brava are unlikely to have been ignored by the richer Romans, who elsewhere in the Mediterranean have shown, beyond doubt, that they had an eye for a good site, and probably many Roman villas of the Empire period remain to be discovered here.

Below Gerona, some 20 kms. down the main Barcelona road, a road (C. 250) leads off to the left down to the coast at San Feliu de Guixols: a short way down this road, to the east of the railway, stands Caldas de Malavella, famous for its medicinal waters in Roman days and now occupied in the mineral water industry. The baths are situated at two separate places: at Puig de las Animas there is left that part of the baths that was the 'frigidarium', measuring 24 feet by 14 feet 6 inches. On three sides are stone steps, each step 14 inches high. The other, more important baths were built adjoining the spring called Els Bullidors. Here is a section of two parallel galleries divided by a line of pillars: there are obviously various rooms besides: one with perforations in the vaulting above must have been the 'tepidarium': there are six baths, one of them, the 'frigidarium', a large one measuring 30 feet by 26 feet 6 inches, with a bank of five steps round three sides of it. This bath is in a rectangular chamber with a portico down one side, through which access is obtained to a long, narrow room containing three small baths which may have been for individual and private use. Mainly stonework is used throughout.

A few kilometres north of Barcelona, adjacent to the main road, the location of the small Roman township of Baetulo was discovered in the immediate vicinity of the parish church of Badalona. Although it is clear from finds of pottery that it existed for the full span of the Roman occupation of Spain, it never rivalled

Barcino in size and did not share in the later development of its neighbour. None the less, excavations in 1934 produced some interesting results. A section of the north-east wall was unearthed, 6 feet in height and more than 4 feet wide. A square tower projected outwards at a gateway, 10 feet wide: the gate itself had been hinged on the side of the tower. Despite the fact that the construction was manifestly Roman workmanship, there were no proper foundations to the wall and the second century B.C. has been assigned to it as the date of origin.

Even in its Latin form the name Barcelona has carried in its first syllable a reminder of the Carthaginian family of Barca, whose implacable hostility to Rome through two generations had, under Hannibal, put the Romans to their severest test. But in the long history of the city's expansion to its present population of 1,300,000, little that is Roman has survived. The oldest part of the city lies between the Plaza de Cataluna and the harbour, and it is here that the few survivals are to be found. Of the original defence wall which formed an ellipse, as is revealed from the air by existing streets, the two half-circular towers that flanked the main gate, still stand in the Plaza Nueva which is approached by the Calle de Puertaferissa leading off from the Ramblas de Estudios.

A little further down the Ramblas in the direction of the harbour, near the Boqueria on the left, is the supposed site of an amphitheatre: but the strongest evidence may well be merely the fact that locally the district is still known as the 'arenaria'. More concrete is the evidence of the existence of a Roman temple, but not sufficient to reveal the identity of the deity to whom it was dedicated, although Hercules has been mentioned. Inside the patio of a medieval building, used as the Excursion Centre of Catalonia, that stands behind the apsidal end of the Cathedral, three Corinthian columns of stone still stand supporting a section of the entablature, representing one corner of a temple. Not far away in the Plaza del Rey is another complete column, having been transferred there by the authorities of the local Archaeological Museum. All four pillars are fluted. In 1836 there were six such columns and these combined with excavations of that date enabled an architect named Antonio Celles to sketch plans of the completed temple which are kept in the Diputación alongside the Cathedral. These show a hexastyle and peripteral temple set on a high base or platform.

At one end of the Calle de los Condes de Barcelona a basilica has recently been discovered: finds from this and other Roman sites are housed in the Casa Padellas (History Museum) in the Plaza del Rey on the opposite side of the Cathedral to the Diputación. Below the Casa a small section of the inner side of the old walls of the city has been laid bare. During the Civil War the destruction of a convent in a narrow street adjoining the Cathedral led to the discovery of a section of the Roman forum. Among a number of pedestals found in the vicinity, one originally bore an equestrian statue of the Emperor Caracalla.

Thirty kilometres to the north of Barcelona on Route C 1413 is the small town of Caldas de Montbuy, where there may be seen the 'frigidarium' of a Roman bath that is so similar to the one just described at Caldas de Malavella as not to warrant the repetition of the details. Forty kilometres further north on the direct route to Puigcerda stands the town of Vich, known to the Romans as Ausa. Here in the patio of the castillo (castle) of Muncada stand the considerable remains of a Roman temple, again of unknown dedication. The style is typically Roman: there were six Corinthian pillars along the front with one at each side between the 'antae' and the end pillar, making eight in all. The pilasters marking the 'antae' are still there. The columns are estimated to have been 20 feet high: the platform base of the temple, nearly 5 feet high, retains its cornice and is of dressed stone: the cella has walls 1 yard thick which are thought originally to have had a plaster finish: it measures about 12 yards and 'long and short' work is prominent on the exterior. A small side door gives access to a vaulted passage beneath the base, where there is a well—perhaps a sacred well that was not unconnected with the dedication of the temple.

Near Manresa a few kilometres north of the monastery of Montserrat stands a mausoleum known by the name of the Torre del Breny. It is in the form of the 'cella' of a temple and, mounted on a tall base, measures 34 feet in height and 29 feet in length. Built of cut stone, it once had mouldings, frieze and cornice: but these are now almost weathered away.

More than halfway back on the road from Montserrat, in the town of Martorell, is a bridge, the Puente del Diablo, which once, like the one at St. Chaumas in Provence, had two commemorative arches spanning the roadway, one at each end. Unhappily, only sufficient of them is left to show that they were of the type with single arcade. Spanning the main road, 20 kms. short of Tarragona, impressive in its stark and baffling isolation, the Arco de Bara has been standing more than eighteen hundred years, sentinel like, to remind the traveller that he is approaching one of the great capitals of Imperial Rome. It is an arch that repays a pause for inspection: for it is the best of its kind in Spain. Roman arches are often described as triumphal, but with the exception of those in Rome itself, where triumphs were staged, the description can be misleading. In the provinces, at any rate, it is more accurate to look upon them as doing honour to a man in his lifetime or commemorating him after his death. In many instances they were intended to be merely pedestals for a statue of the person honoured. An inscription on the frieze of this particular one tells us that it was erected to the memory of Lucius Licinius Sura, one of Trajan's generals at the end of the first century A.D., in accordance with the directions of his will. It stands 40 feet high and is adorned by two fluted pilasters of the Corinthian style on each side of the arch.

Twelve kilometres nearer the city, not far from the road, on the hillside, is the great Roman quarry, Cantera del Model: and on the right of the road, a further 2 kms. on, stands a funeral tower, known as the Torre de los Escipiones. Few Romans better deserve to be commemorated in the neighbourhood of Tarragona than 'the two thunderbolts' of the war against Carthage, but the two figures that are carved in relief on the lower section of the tower are, beyond doubt, intended to be slaves and not the two Scipios. Their dress is that of native Iberians and they have cowls on their heads. Between the two figures is a square inset with a very faint inscription, which Hubner in the second half of the nineteenth century identified as the epitaph of a woman called Cornelia, who, in all likelihood, was one of the family of the Scipios. The tower itself took the familiar form of base and two upper sections divided by a moulding: without the top of the upper section, which is missing, it attains a height of 26 feet and is entirely composed of ashlar stone.

For those again who ask why this monument also stands in splendid isolation, the view from it over the city may well be their answer. For Tarragona is nobly set on natural terraces that lead down to the sea. Here it was that Augustus himself, after labouring six long years to create a new world for war-weary Rome, found peace and rest for the seventh. In our own day few writers have failed to fall beneath its spell. 'Tarragona is possibly the most grandly poised city in Europe', writes Miss Macaulay in her *Fabled Shore*. 'The shape formed by the steep walls that encircle it and the climbing mass of the ancient town crowned by the Cathedral on its summit is superb. The imagination, long haunted, is at first glance captured and possessed for ever by this Roman-medieval city.' Mr. Sacheverell Sitwell's *Spain* rightly emphasises the golden light of Tarragona: the light is the bright, clear light of all Spain, here aided and abetted by a mistral from the north-west. The gold is in the yellow stone that built the Roman camp and the medieval cathedral that now stands within its walls.

Scipio's first Roman camp (*c.* 218 B.C.) on the hill-top was limited in space by the existing defences of the Iberian community that had already occupied it through successive generations for three or four hundred years. Much of the lower recesses of the wall that can be seen today is composed of massive masonry of cyclopean proportions: the smaller stone of the Romans surmounts it, topped in its turn by medieval work. Owing to the fact that it is an adaptation of existing pre-Roman defences, this camp can never have

PLAN OF TARRAGONA
ROMAN SITES
MODERN TOWN
A ROMANO-IBERIAN WALLS
B SITE OF CIRCUS
C SITE OF BASILICA
D SITE OF FORUM
E AMPHITHEATRE
F SO-CALLED PALACE OF AUGUSTUS
G ROMANO-CHRISTIAN NECROPOLIS
H SITE OF THEATRE
J SITE OF TEMPLE OF JUPITER
K SITE OF TEMPLE OF AUGUSTUS
L VIA TRIUMPHALIS
M TEMPLE (OF MINERVA ?)
N REMAINS OF ARCHES
O SITE OF TEMPLE DEDICATION UNKNOWN)
N
RAMBLA DEL GENERALISIMO
MEDITERRANEAN SEA
0 100 200 300 400 500m

had the traditional rectangular shape with four gates. These walls are pierced by five entrances of pre-Roman date and what is now styled the Roman Imperial gate is in the centre of the north-east side, remote from the town. But the wall on the opposite side—the side of the town—was quite soon removed, because the area enclosed by the Iberian defences was too small for Roman purposes and, once the war with Carthage was over the need for them would appear to be gone.

Halfway along the Paseo Arqueslogico, that permits the public to walk around the outside of the walls, stands a statue of Augustus, presented to the town by the Italian Government in 1934. The so-called palace of Augustus is the tall, rectangular building adjacent to the south-eastern end of the wall: it is stone-built and one of its façades reveals a series of Tuscan pilasters: the interior still retains a vaulted nave. This building was the praetorium or headquarters of the military commander and may have housed the praetorian guard as well.

The temple of Augustus which Tiberius gave the citizens permission to build in A.D. 16, and that of Jupiter-Ammon are lost beneath the foundations of the present Cathedral, but evidence about the one comes from an unusual source—from Tarragona coins. These show on the one side Augustus seated with victory in his hand, on the other side, his temple, octostyle and peripteral with a medallion in the centre of the triangular gable: from the actual remains of its Corinthian columns, its height—not counting the base on which it stood—is assessed as about 38 feet. The adjacent temple of Jupiter-Ammon is not thought to have been quite so high. Capitals of mixed Corinthian-Ionic order, belonging to it, were found in the course of work on the Seminary behind the Cathedral. tions of the frieze have been preserved represen sacerdotal mitre and instruments of sacrifices set tween garlands; and two medallions, each bearing th head of Jupiter-Ammon, probably belonged to the pediments.

The Calle Mayor that leads down from the steps of the Cathedral was the main street of the Roman city, its counterpart in crosswise direction being the Calle de Caballeros: to the north of the Calle Mayor lay the forum, arches that led to the western entrance of it being discovered in the Plaza Pallol. Surprisingly, next to the forum and more or less parallel with it, but on a lower terrace, was the circus that occupied the stretch between the City Hall and the Charles V Tower. Its dimensions were 390 yards by 110 yards if plans of it made in the eighteenth century are to be relied upon. A little of the vaulting that supported the seats is still to be seen: the more interesting are at the south end of the Calle Euladrillado, near the Palacio de Augusto: others are beneath the stairs of the Bajada de Misericordia at the lower end of the Calle Mayor. The 'carceres', or starting gate, was where the City Hall now stands. The triumphal gate through which the winner passed to receive the plaudits of the assembled company does not, in this instance, appear to have been in its traditional place, halfway along the semicircular end, because it was there that the platform reserved for the presiding magistrate was found. But about halfway along what used to be the long south-west side of the circus is a street called Portalet, which may well mark the place where the triumphal gate was.

The site of the amphitheatre is not difficult to find,

since it lies on the foreshore, short of the railway, and is visible from the Paseo de Calvo Sotelo, a promenade overlooking the sea, that starts to the left where the Barcelona road enters the town at the southern end of the Rambla de San Carlos. Measuring 140 yards by 110 yards, it gives a good overall impression of its original state. Although the work on it—financed, incidentally, by an American millionaire—seems to be mainly excavation, it is clear that it was built in the familiar style on vaulted arches. The 'podium' that enclosed the arena is much in evidence. Some literary evidence of the sixteenth century speaks of the portico round the upper tier of seats as having Tuscan columns. This amphitheatre at Tarragona is surely unique in having had a church at a later date built in the centre of its arena: this is a Romanesque church of the eleventh century, and, being also in ruins, should not be taken to be part of the normal embellishments of an amphitheatre. It was dedicated to Santa Maria del Milagro, but if there were any justice or sentiment in history, it would be dedicated to the canonised Bishop Fructuosus of Tarragona, who was burnt at the stake on this very spot in the persecutions of A.D. 258, after suffering imprisonment in the Palacio de Augusto which virtually overlooks it.

The present population of the city is in the neighbourhood of forty thousand, while thirty thousand has been given for the figures during its palmiest days under the Empire. If this estimate is accepted, it follows that the city occupied a very considerable portion of its present area, and this is confirmed by discoveries in recent years well away from the ancient citadel at the top of the hill. In the Calle Cervantes, about 300 yards to the south of the broad Rambla del

Arch at Capera

Generalissimo, just beyond the main post office, a second forum has been unearthed, including a row of columns—between which once stood shops—several private houses, the carriage-way of a Roman street, water-supply systems and valuable specimens of architectural sculpture. State funds are being made available for further work in the immediate area. Important finds had, however, been made before in this district, which had, at least, established the existence of baths and gymnasium and of temples dedicated to Venus, Minerva, Isis and Mithras. It was customary to establish the cult of these latter two in residential districts well away from official headquarters.

It was also not far from here that a theatre was located, adjoining the Calle Mayor: the remains were fragmentary, but sufficient to establish that the theatre had been a large one. A small section of the seating remained with vaulting to support it. A modern building made it impossible to excavate the stage; but three of the statues that once adorned it were found, as was the usual inscription relating to the allocation of seats by social rank. A second inscription starts the title of an emperor, but unhappily it is incomplete: the style of the lettering, however, suggests the second century A.D., which would match with the comparatively suburban site of the theatre. But if Cadiz had a theatre as early as 50 B.C., this can scarcely be Tarragona's first theatre. A third inscription was dedicated to the tutelary goddess of one Aemilius Severianus, an actor.

The provincial Archaeological Museum is housed in the lower reaches of the City Hall and any such collection in Tarragona is obviously worth a visit. Among the many fine specimens of statuary may be mentioned that of Bacchus in the style of Praxiteles and sculptured marble busts of Marcus Aurelius, Trajan and Hadrian: also there is a beautiful ivory doll, 10 inches high and articulated, believed to be the work of the fourth century: it is found buried with a little girl of about six years of age.

There is a second museum in the Paseo de Independencia which turns left off the high-road to Valencia just short of the bridge over the river Francoli. This museum is linked with the early Christian cemetery found here in 1923: marble or stone sarcophagi dating from the third century onwards are on view, with coffins of wood and lead and graves of tiles or brick. But the exhibition is not entirely devoted to the apparatus of death. There is a display besides of glass and ceramic ware, pagan and Christian inscriptions, mosaics and coins.

Four kilometres north of Tarragona near the road that leads to Valls and Lerida is found the 'Puente de las Ferreras', an aqueduct that was part of the system that brought water to the city over a distance of almost 16 miles. There are two rows of arches, eleven in the lower and twenty-five in the top. It is nearly 220 yards long and its greatest height is 80 feet. In contrast with the aqueduct at Segovia, the thickness of the lower sections of pillars detracts from the proportions of the whole.

Not far away in the valley of the Francoli is the little village of Constanti, 5 or 6 kms. from the city. Some 2 kms. further on, at the end of a rough track, is a group of buildings under the name of Centcellas, which has so far baffled the experts. Attempts to identify it have varied from Byzantine basilica to soldiers' barracks. The main premises consist of a square building —with a second roofless one attached to it—and are in use as a farmhouse. The ground-floor room, circular on the inside, has four niches in the wall: upstairs, on the hemispherical ceiling is the finest mosaic of its type in Spain, with representations of hunting-scenes and various figures and buildings. The roofless section adjoining is rectangular, with four projecting recesses in the walls: of the other buildings only odd pieces of wall and vaulting remain. The mosaic is judged to be fourth-century work: but coins of the reign of Hadrian have been found on the site. The circular room could very well have been the 'frigidarium' of baths that were part of a luxury villa of the Empire period. The distance from Tarragona and the general situation of the estate would be appropriate for such a residence. But until further excavations are made, identification must remain a matter of conjecture.

Last of the Roman monuments in the Tarragona district to be mentioned is the mausoleum at Vilarrodona, north-east of Valls. It takes the now familiar form of a rectangular temple with Tuscan pilasters in its walls. Built in a combination of brick and stone, it is not in a good state of preservation: mouldings of both the inside and outside have almost entirely disappeared. One peculiarity, however, it does have, since it was obviously a 'columbarium': for inside the 'cella' can still be seen the pigeon-holes for the reception of cinerary urns.

One hundred kilometres north-west of Tarragona, but still within the limits of Catalonia, is Lerida, which under the name of Ilerda figured prominently in Caesar's first campaign in Spain during the Civil War. Its main direct link with Roman times was the bridge over the river Segre, which, although heavily restored, retained more of the original stonework than either of the other two Roman bridges in Catalonia. Unfortunately, it was seriously damaged in the Civil War of 1936-1939. A few kilometres upstream at Corbins the ruins of a mausoleum in temple form may be seen: the 'cella' is square-shaped and once had a vaulted roof; the subterranean chamber was also vaulted and is divided into four sections—each 4 feet wide—for the committal of the dead.

A spot 5 kms. north of the picturesque pueblo of Fraga, which is itself 31 kms. west of Lerida on the main highway to Saragossa, has been the scene of two separate investigations. The second, in 1942, was under the direction of Dr. J. C. Serra-Rafols. A vast Roman country house was laid bare, revealing three distinct styles of construction. The main feature is the traditional atrium, which, measuring 65 feet by 56 feet, would be more correctly called a peristyle. The rooms on the north, east and south sides are all of one period, late third century A.D., after the first Germanic raid into Spain, and represent an extension of the original premises, which are found at a lower level on the west side, grouped round an atrium of more normal proportions. A date as early as the second century A.D. is assigned to these.

When Christianity was accepted, the owner decided to have his name Fortunatus, in conjunction with a Christian symbol, incorporated into a new mosaic floor in one of the rooms to the south of the peristyle, and the whole villa is now known by this name. Whether he proceeded to build the Christian chapel that was found in the south-west corner of the site, encroaching to some extent on the oldest part of the villa centred on the small atrium, is another question. It is, however, quite definite that the chapel was in use after the villa ceased to be inhabited, because several of the rooms had been used for Christian burials. It is surmised that the villa was rendered uninhabitable by the final Germanic raids early in the fifth century, and that the chapel, whatever the date of its origin, survived through the Visigothic period until the arrival of the Moors in the eighth century.

The chapel, which lies almost due north and south and occupies an area nearly as large as the peristyle, is rectangular, with a small square projection on the north side, which on the inside ends in an apsidal curve. Beneath this area was a crypt, the steps to which lead down from a place in the centre of the nave, the main body of the building. The south end of the rectangle is occupied by various antechambers fulfilling the general purpose of a narthex.

A short distance downstream from Lerida, below the junction with the Segre, the river Ebro receives another tributary, the Matarrana, and it is near this latter river that there is found at Fabara as well-preserved a mausoleum as any in Spain. It is in the form of a tetrastyle temple. The four columns along the front are of the Tuscan order and have smooth pillars. By way of contrast, the pilasters inserted into the sides of the 'cella' are fluted. The entablature is Ionic in style, decorated by a simple pattern in relief and in the pediment above is an inscription that says that the building is dedicated to the 'Manes' (departed spirit) of one Lucius Aemilius Lupus. Inside the 'cella' immediately to the left on entrance, is a stairway leading down to the vaulted sepulchral crypt below. The stonework throughout is large-section ashlar, laid without cement, but here and there reinforced by iron bars.

The next Roman monument is well down the Via

Augusta at the little community of Cabanes, not on the modern coast road, but on one that runs more or less parallel with it, a few kilometres inland from Oropesa. Here an arch spans a short section of the Roman road. Two stout pillars supported the superstructure of which only the voussoirs of the arch remain, giving a naked, not to mention precarious, look to the whole. There is no evidence of date, but the style of stonework suggests an early one.

The Roman theatre at Sagunto (21 kms. north of Valencia) is smaller than the one at Merida: but its situation is much more dramatic, as it is set into the north side of the steep hill on the top of which stood the original fortified town of the Iberians. Livy's account of the taking of this town in 219 B.C. by Hannibal is cast in terms that very properly invite sympathy for the beleaguered Saguntines and for their most gallant resistance that ended amid scenes of unforgettable heroism. But acquaintance with the local topography of Saguntum is likely also to create a healthy regard for the forces of Hannibal, partly Carthaginians, partly Spaniards, who manhandled their battering rams, their penthouses, their 'tabulata' and their engines of war up these formidable slopes before they could even begin to mount an attack on the actual defences. Long before the theatre was built, history herself had staged a drama in this place as grim as any that was ever in later years presented on its boards.

Naturally, a larger proportion than usual of the seating accommodation of this theatre is built on to the solid hillside, and it was the stage that was in need of artificial reinforcement. The stone dressing of the rows of seats has largely disappeared, but the outlines remain reasonably clear. In front are the three rows for the chairs of the authorities: behind and above rise three sections of seats—comprising six, seven and ten rows respectively—divided each from the other by a gangway for the passage of spectators. Seven stairways can be traced mounting upwards and outwards through the seats: the final section of the seating—rows twenty-seven and upwards—are built upon a gallery above a substantial wall, pierced by six doorways that lead to the outside: what looks like the pedestal for a statue is set in the centre of this wall, breaking the line of it.

The stage was built on the top of vaulting that sprang from a series of parallel walls: it was 165 feet long and 20 feet wide: of the traditional permanent set and of the actors' premises to the rear of it, nothing has survived. Underneath the orchestra and through the foundations of the stage runs a drain.

A certain Miguel Arnao constructed two models of this theatre in 1796; they are kept respectively in the Archaeological Museums of Valencia and Madrid: incidentally, many of the smaller Roman finds at Sagunto are to be seen in a museum that is housed in the entrance of the castle at the top of the hill above the theatre.

Down near the river Palancia are the remains of a circus that was nearly 300 yards long and more than 70 yards wide. A section of wall down one side, including a gateway, is left, and sufficient of the 'spina' or central ridge to show that it was just over 4 feet in height: the triumphal gate was in the usual place, in the centre of the semicircular end. A new school is being erected on part of the site.

Despite the importance to the Romans of Valencia, which they founded in 138 B.C., and even more of

Cartagena, which for a while, at first, was the capital of Hither Spain, there are no major Roman monuments surviving in the coastal region between Saguntum and the statue of Janus that stood on the Via Augusta to mark the boundary line between Tarraconensis and Baetica. That is not to say, of course, that impressive Roman structures never existed in these regions. For instance, it is known that the cult of the goddess Diana was popular throughout the whole district. There was a temple dedicated to her in Saguntum itself which was matched by a temple of Venus at Almenara, a bare kilometre from the sea, not far from the town. In the hinterland, adjoining the ruins of Ercavica (Cabeza del Griego) at the head of the Tagus valley, there was a shrine of Diana: on a vertical section of rock, that may once have served as the end wall of some building, are carved representations of Diana, together with dedicatory inscriptions. Still more famous and ancient was Diana's temple at Dianium, the town which took its name from her and is now the flourishing little port of Denia, halfway between Valencia and Alicante. Unhappily, this temple and the two at or near Saguntum are little more than bare outlines, but undoubtedly excavation would produce details of construction and age.

It is no surprise to record villa sites in this favoured part of Spain: one at Ador in the province of Valencia: a second was found as long ago as 1777 at Puig de Cebolla near Valencia itself: several square chambers were unearthed, paved either with mosaics or marble. Thirty years or more ago at Purol 'in agro Saguntino' several villas or granges were revealed, some of them showing 'patio' and 'impluvium'. One of them is reminiscent of the Roman villa at Chedworth, near

Cirencester, in that it combined business and residential premises. On the south side is a large chamber 39 feet by 22 feet where the process of winepressing was carried on. Correspondingly on the north side was an olive mill: two enormous round millstones were found *in situ*. A similar hint of a livelihood being earned is conveyed by the fishponds found on the headland of San Antonio below Denia. Such ponds in the living rock could be of any age: but here the supplementary stonework is undoubtedly Roman.

Further down the coast at Villajoyosa there is a sepulchral tower known locally as the Torre de San José. Measuring just over 4 yards by 3 yards, the base is composed of four steps from which rises one section only of tower: the two sides are relieved by pilasters and a door in the front leads to a small vaulted interior with a small, low window at the far end. A similar kind of structure, the Torre Ciega, stands one kilometre north of the railway station in Cartagena: if genuine, it is a relic from a Roman necropolis: local lore insists that this too is the tomb of a Scipio.

The Balearic Islands were included in the historical review of the mainland, and since their Roman monuments scarcely warrant a separate section, they are as well considered here as anywhere. The two large islands each had a theatre: for the one on Minorca there is only the evidence of inscriptions: but at Alcudia in the north of Majorca there is something more definite. It was quite a small theatre: the first two rows for the authorities and the 4-foot gangway behind it are readily discernible, as are the next eight rows above, divided regularly into four 'cunei' or wedges by three ascending stairways: a short piece of wall marks the position of the back stage set.

Apart from traces of burials in the small caves, in which the islands abound, Roman remains are hard to find. There were only two actual Roman settlements in Majorca, Palmaria (Campos) and Pollentia (Alcudia) and a further two in Minorca, in Mahon and near Ciudadela. So, while there is ample evidence still of the smaller articles of trade in all parts of the islands, major Roman works were obviously limited in number.

CHAPTER XI

Tarraconensis (continued)

THE idea of Madrid as the hub of communications for Spain was not a Roman conception, but the product of strong nationalistic sentiment in the sixteenth century. It was no business of the Romans to encourage patriotic feeling, in any way, on a local scale: so it can be said that metaphorically, in their day, all roads led to Rome. In a more literal sense, in relation to the modern capital, the Roman roads of the Peninsula formed the square frame of a picture of which Madrid, had it then existed, would have been the centre. There was, however, one major, diagonal road that ran from Merida via Toledo and Alcala de Henares to Saragossa: so that, of the many roads that now radiate from Madrid through what was the ancient province of Tarraconensis, it is the road to Saragossa that is likely to reveal surviving associations with imperial Rome. But first, Toledo!

Toledo, known to the Romans as Toletum, had been the tribal centre of the Oretani from before the time the Carthaginians arrived in Spain about 500 B.C. It stands, as it has always stood, in a tight loop of the river Tagus that flows round three sides of it in a deep ravine; by nature, therefore, a strong defensive position whose worth has been proved even under some of the conditions of modern warfare as recently as the

Civil War of 1936-1939. Toledo never achieved under the Romans that pre-eminence in Spanish affairs that it did later under the Visigoths and Moors and, after the eleventh century, as the capital of Castile. To the Romans it was a tribal centre that, under their policy of urbanisation in the early stages of the Empire, was due to have grafted upon it those civic amenities that were calculated to woo the local inhabitants from their barbarous ways. Some of these amenities have in part —a small part—survived.

The circus lies to the north of the town, near the well-known restaurant of Venta Aires: the site of the arena is occupied by public gardens: near the chapel of the Cristo de la Vega is the arch of a lateral entrance with a section of the gallery that ran beneath the seating. The top of the arch of the triumphal gate at the semicircular end projects above ground level: the 'spina' is not visible. It is calculated that the circus was almost a quarter of a mile long and more than 100 yards broad.

On the same side of the town, on the right-hand side of the Madrid road, beyond the junction formed by the road to Avila, is the district called Las Covachuelas—The Vaulted Corridors. But whether these signify the onetime presence on this spot of theatre or amphitheatre, it is not possible to establish. It is said that there was once definite evidence of a theatre: but, owing to the restricted amount of open ground, there may have been both theatre and amphitheatre, close together, as at Merida.

About 1924 a Roman villa was found on land belonging to the Fabrica de Armas—the factory associated with the production of Toledo swords—which stands a short distance out near the Madrid road. One room that was excavated had had a fountain and was thought to have been a 'triclinium'. It led on to the 'atrium', where the 'impluvium' was octagonal with a tessellated floor.

The two older of the three bridges across the Tagus are Roman in foundation, and some stonework of their period of origin is still visible in them. The oldest is the one nearest to the railway station and is called the Puente de Alcantara. It should not be confused with its namesake, one of Spain's most impressive Roman structures, on the borders of Portugal.

Apart from Segovia, whose aqueduct, described in a previous chapter, should not be missed, there is nothing else Roman within the compass of a day's journey from the capital. But the sombre magnificence of the Escorial monastery, set at a height of nearly 3,000 feet in the Guadarramas, is, by the derivation of its name from the Latin word 'scoria' (a slag tip), a reminder that the Romans once mined these hills.

However, 150 kms. along the road to Saragossa, the small township of Medinaceli—Oscilis, to the Romans—still retains a notable memorial arch. Like the arches of Septimus Severus and Constantine in Rome, it has a large central arch for wheeled traffic, flanked on each side by a smaller arch for pedestrians. It is made of dressed stone and is in quite a good state of preservation. Two horizontal mouldings, the lower of which is interrupted by the tall central arch, divide the height of the structure into three sections, not counting the base. The two small arches, built through the pillars of the main arch, are confined by the lower mouldings to the first section. Directly above them, in the centre section, one on each side of the semicircular central arch, are two pairs of Corinthian pilasters, supporting gables, framing rectangular spaces that were intended to contain figures in relief. A series of holes in the frieze reveals that the letters of the dedicating inscription were in bronze: but it is not possible on such flimsy evidence to reconstitute the original words. The general style of the monument, however, suggests that it does, at least, date from the time of the Empire. Built at a point more than 4,000 feet above sea-level, it commands a wide and impressive view over wild hills and valleys.

Some 40 kms. further along the road, near Santa Maria de Huerta, a Roman house of such proportions was laid bare in the ruins of Arcobriga as to merit the description of either a small palace or praetorium (official residence). Some weight is lent to the second conjecture by the fact that the building directly opposite appears to have been a barracks or guard house. The residence was a typical Roman house on a large scale. A passage led from the street into a columnated patio, surrounding which were the tabularium (record office), dining-room and bedrooms. However, from the patio a stairway led down to a terrace where the domestic quarters and storehouses were sited: kitchens were identified and an oven for bread-making. From the remnants of mouldings and plaster, it was evident that the main rooms had been lavishly decorated, in Pompeian style, with paintings of fruits and flowers. Despite their comparative proximity to each other, both Arcobriga and Bilbilis—the birthplace of the poet Martial, 6 kms. from Calatayud—had theatres. Neither has received much attention, but there is sufficient evidence to show that the theatre at Bilbilis was not a small one.

Apart from incorporating in its name the identity of its founder, Caesar Augustus, the large modern city of Saragossa no longer has any direct links with its Roman past, apart from some fragments of the wall and a tower in the garden of the convent of San Sepulcro near the eastern river bridge which carries the Barcelona road. In fact, the site of the Roman walled town was alongside this city bank of the river. The Calle Don Jaime I, leading into the city from the west bridge, was the one main street, the Calle Mayor the other that crossed it at right angles. The walls themselves were demolished during the siege of 1808, but their outline is traced by the Paseo del Ebro, the Calle del Coso, the Calle de Cerdan and the Plaza de Lanuza. The two Augustan gates—de Toledo and de Valencia—were pulled down in 1842 and 1859 respectively. A roughly inscribed stone in the latter made it clear that Italian workmen had been engaged on its construction.

The upper reaches of the Ebro are not as rewarding in the matter of Roman monuments as the corresponding section of the Douro that runs almost parallel in the opposite direction, to the south of it. But the small township of Sadaba, now remote from modern communications in the valley of the Arba, once stood nearly halfway along the Roman highway that went from Saragossa to Pamplona and, possibly through its very remoteness, has preserved at least three direct links with Rome. A large number of stone-built pillars provide unmistakable evidence of a Roman aqueduct. In a quarter of the town with the significant name of Los Bañales the ruins of Roman baths may be seen: walls and springers of vaulting are present in sufficient quantity to make it possible to identify the different departments.

But most striking of the three is the façade of the

mausoleum, built, probably in the second century, for members of the Atilii family. It stands on a heavy base of three layers of massive, uncemented masonry and it is divided by six pilasters of composite Corinthian-Ionian order into five blind doorways: doorways one, three and five project slightly in front of numbers two and four and are crowned each with a small pediment: the pillars of the pilasters are adorned with carving of unusual richness and each of the five doors has carved on it, in relief, a hanging loop that completes the circle of the upper section of arched doorway. Here once rested the busts of the persons honoured by the monument. The dedicatory details are inscribed along the frieze: amongst other things, they reveal that the mausoleum was erected under the direction and at the expense of a woman.

Calahorra, 49 kms. short of Logroño on the road from Saragossa, as Calagurris, the scene of much hard fighting between Sertorius and Pompey, still retains signs of a circus and an amphitheatre. The circus lies to the east of the town and measured some 490 yards by 116 yards. When Cean Bermudez was conducting his review of Spanish antiquities in 1832, most of the seating was still in position. The amphitheatre is less definite, only the barest outline existing to reveal the site.

At a point about halfway between Calahorra and Saragossa a Roman road left the right bank of the Ebro, crossed over into the head-waters of the Douro and passing through the townships of Augustobriga (Agreda), Numantia, Uxama (Burgos de Osma) turned northwest to reach Clunia (Coruña del Conde) and thereafter followed the right bank of the Douro until it reached the main Astorga-Merida highway at Ocelodurum (Zamora), north of the boundaries of Lusitania.

Merida. Aerial view showing Circus (top left) and Amphitheatre and Theatre (bottom centre) in descending order

Merida. Los Milagros Aqueduct

All the above towns still retain traces of Roman occupation.

At Agreda it is still possible to see the outlines of the Roman walls, which take the shape of a large and irregular polygon. Quite substantial sections of it remain, some of it revealing up to four or five layers of dressed stonework, representing the exterior facing of the wall. The inner side had a much rougher finish.

The walls of Numantia are not so complete in outline; but there is one section worth mentioning, some 50 yards long, in the southern half of the town: it attains, roughly, the same height as the wall at Agreda, but it also includes a rectangular tower in its length. Incidentally, Numantia is best approached from the neighbouring town of Soria. Cross the bridge over the Douro on the east of the town and turning left, follow the road to Garray, 7 kms. away. The ruins of Numantia lie on adjacent high ground: an obelisk has been raised to commemorate the final gallant siege that the town endured in 133 B.C. The shape of the town was decided, in the main, by the contours of the top of the hill and may best be described as an ellipse, some 450 yards long at its widest and 325 yards across the shorter diameter.

Apart from the wall, the ruins comprise several narrow streets intersecting at right angles. The houses whose outlines are revealed are of especial interest because they are, in the main, the dwellings of the pre-Roman Numantines, and are planned in a style that has little in common with the typical Roman house. One particular feature of them is a cellar, 9 or 10 feet deep, square or rectangular in shape, lined with stone and built underneath the house, near the street entrance. It is supposed that these subterranean chambers were provision stores. A second point of interest is the method adopted to collect water, a service performed in houses of Roman design by an 'impluvium'. Here wells are commonly found in front of houses, with channels carefully designed to carry the overflow under the footpath into the gutter. In one street that falls away towards the western end of the town a four-sided drain, made of flagstones, was laid bare, running beneath the entire length of one pavement for a distance of more than 100 yards. Two of the buildings served by it were probably public baths, one for each sex; the hypocaust of the one survives and, of the other, the cement flooring of a bath.

All the houses in the Numantine style are small and unimpressive: as, indeed, are the few later houses, built in the Roman manner, some time after the destruction of the town in 133 B.C. For never afterwards did Numantia amount to anything more than a village. In the western section, however, there is one where the entrance passage, patio and side-rooms are identifiable: at the far end of the patio was a kitchen with a round fireplace in the centre. There is a second house to match this one towards the northern part of the town: in this case, it can be seen that there were eight columns standing round the patio. These columns are not an isolated instance. There are others to be found along the front of the façade of a building in one of the main streets.

Towards the south end of the town the ground falls away, and where a block of houses extended from one street to another parallel with it, the normal entrance was from the higher street and the rear premises were built in two storeys with, however, no apparent means of exit to the lower street. In at least three houses the patio was found on the lower level, communicating with the front premises by means of a stone stairway. None of the Roman houses in Numantia betrays any signs of great affluence: not a single complete pavement of mosaic has been found, cement or stone slabs being substituted. Such mural paintings as have been discovered, had red as their basic colour and were of the simplest, not to say crude, design.

Archaeological interest is not, however, centred exclusively upon the town. For in the immediate neighbourhood are relics of the oldest Roman camps in Western Europe, those, in fact, that were built in the prolonged campaign against the Celtiberi which ended with the destruction of Numantia in 133 B.C. There are two groups of these camps: one, the earlier in date, is found on the top of a hill near the little village of Renieblas, 6 kms. east of Numantia, and is an amalgam of five different camps superimposed in turn, one upon another, at varying dates. The identification of these camps was the work of Professor Schulten of Barcelona University. The earliest of them was that constructed in 153 B.C. by Fulvius Nobilior, whose summer camp of that same year can still be traced at Almazan, halfway along the road from the south, from Medinaceli; the other four are later reconstructions and amplifications of it and the largest of them is almost exactly 1,000 yards long. The walls are of stone and are 3 yards in thickness. Square towers, which were incorporated in them at intervals, projected on the inside of the wall only. Within the camp itself the foundations are visible of the barracks—long, parallel buildings divided into square rooms: also identifiable are the sites of the officers' quarters, and of the stores.

In general, the Numantine camps conform closely with the description given by Polybius of the typical Roman camp of these days. Very briefly, such a camp was virtually square, with a gate in each of the four sides: porta Praetoria at the front, porta decumana at the rear. Porta dextra and porta sinistra were in their respective sides and were linked across the camp by a road—the via principalis, which divided the officers' quarters from the barracks of the men: the latter were often divided into two sections by another road—the via quintana—which ran parallel with the via principalis. One of the camps at Renieblas reflects these arrangements precisely, revealing the accommodation for a legion divided into six sections, each section with ten barracks, five each side of the via quintana. Men were assigned their barracks, and even the rooms inside the barracks, in such a way as to preserve their military formation. Thus, in an emergency, it was easy for a legion to fall in with the minimum of disorder and confusion.

Two of the camps that protrude beyond the limits of the actual hill appear to have been occupied by an army of occupation, for coins have been found there of a date later than the taking of the town. The arrangement of the quarters in the fifth and latest encampment suggested to Professor Schulten a date for its construction later than the reforms of the army that Marius put through round about 95 B.C.

The second group of camps is that incorporated in the ring of defences that Scipio Aemilianus had erected round the town of Numantia in the course of the siege that led to its capture in 133 B.C. In spite of the fact that they were intended for use over a limited period only, the fortifications were stone-built; their chief features today are two camps, one to the south-east of the town on a hill called Peña Redonda: the other, half a mile to the north on a site that goes under the name of Castillejo. The latter was the headquarters of Scipio himself, the former under the command of his brother. Neither camp preserves the traditional lay-out of a Roman camp and no attempt was made to impose the accepted design on the difficult terrain, as had been done with such success at Renieblas.

The camp at Peña Redonda is more than 600 yards long and its width varies between 110 yards and 180 yards. The main praetorian gate is well defined—16 feet wide—flanked with towers: the barrack buildings are 16 yards wide and vary in length between 65 yards and 100 yards; in each case they are divided by a long wall down the middle and the two halves thus formed are in turn partitioned off into smaller rooms. It is calculated that there was accommodation in the camp for a legion at the full strength of 4,200 men.

Castillejo, to the north, commands a wide view over the country to the east of Numantia and in the course of the war had found favour as a strategic site with Marcellus in 151 B.C. and again with Pompeius in 141 B.C. There was, therefore, a degree of permanency attached to it that caused Scipio, seven years later, to select it as his headquarters for his siege of the town. In fact, the quarters used by him have been identified —a large rectangular room (now, of course, existing only at ground-level) with the base of a column in each corner and halfway down the two longer sides. As a whole, the camp assumed the shape of a trapezium of which the two longer sides extend for some 380 yards and 250 yards respectively. The porta decumana in the rear wall has been located: it was 26 feet wide.

The defensive towers that guarded the porta praetoria have been found and the street that traditionally linked the two gates, still retains its stone surface and its footpaths, although, owing to the unusual shape of the camp, it runs in an irregular line. Even so, the quarters erected for the troops contrived to run in the traditional straight lines and occupy an area almost 200 yards square.

With Castillejo, the catalogue of the relics of militant Rome ceases, at least for the time being. Uxama (Burgo de Osma), with the outlines of the 'cavea' of a theatre engraved on a hillside, reminds us once again of Romans dedicated to the ways of peace and, at the same time, of glories of its own, long departed. The same thoughts might well occur at the next halt westwards down this Roman road, at Clunia (Coruña del Conde). It is not easy in this lonely, deserted place to realise that here the aged Galba communed with himself and later left, perhaps against his better judgement, to salvage what he could of the Roman world from the havoc that Nero made. Today the skeleton of the large auditorium of a theatre lies carved on a gaunt hillside: the view therefrom is no longer at a stage whose structure filled the eye—for only five isolated segments of it remain—but over a wide and distant vista of brightly hued Castilian agriculture, with, as is often the case in the Spanish countryside, no hint of the homes of those who work there: a few windswept trees growing amid the rear premises of the stage add their own incongruous touch.

The three orders of seats can easily be traced, since the parallel passage-ways that separate them are more clearly cut than much of the surviving rows of seats, which, in general, have lost their dressing of stone.

The topmost range of seats was divided by nine stairways, the lower two ranges by five. The stage was more than 50 yards in length: uniformly, through the five sections of its surviving masonry run two lines of holes, marking two storeys. Pieces of Tuscan columns that were found, confirmed the impression that, without doubt, this was once a theatre of some importance.

The rest of Tarraconensis is disappointing in its yield of Roman monuments, even if Portugal north of the Douro be properly included in it. There, Braga admits its identity with Bracara Augusta, but nothing more, but at Chaves (Aquae Flaviae) the ancient bridge of sixteen arches is Roman. The parapets have not stood the test of time and have been substituted by not unattractive railings: in the centre stands a tall, circular monolith with a Latin inscription, reminding the traveller that he is on the road that connects Astorga with Braga.

Again, some 15 kms. from Guimaraes, south-east of Braga, a pre-Roman, hilltop settlement called Citania de Briteiros has had a deal of excavatory work done on it. There are many of these settlements in this part of Portugal and they represent native communities at various stages of Romanisation. Indeed, Castro de Sabroso, only 2 kms. away, yielded no Roman relics of any sort and must have been abandoned before, or at the time that the Romans permanently occupied the district. Citania de Briteiros, on the other hand, had obviously had strong commercial connections with their conquerors: for many small items of Roman manufacture have been found and are kept in the museum at Guimaraes. But the greater interest lies in comparing the primitive type of round, stone-built house found here with the contemporary Celtic square house of the Celtiberi in Numantia, and in realising how little was the effect the Romans had on the way of life of the Lusitanians and Galicians, if they failed to provide new towns on the plains for them to live in.

The same contrast in the style and shape of pre-Roman dwellings is to be seen elsewhere in the province at Coaña, $4\frac{1}{2}$ miles from the small town of Navia in western Asturias and at Azaila, near the Ebro, 60 kms. east of Saragossa. The existence of the former had been known from the early nineteenth century, but it was only in 1939 that a serious attempt was made under the direction of Sr. Uria of Oviedo University to investigate the site effectively. Round houses or hutments were found in plenty, conforming with the description of them given by Strabo, who added that at mealtimes the inhabitants sat round the walls inside and food was handed round. Frequent finds of coins and pottery proved that the little community survived at least to the third century A.D.

The square houses at Azaila, as those of Numantia, reflect the higher standard of civilisation that the Celtic element had brought to the Celtiberi, but even so, they are stone only for the first 3 feet of their height, with adobe for the rest. Azaila had been much the larger place: for the town extended a good way beyond the hill of Cabezo de Alcala which served as an acropolis. Yet it was on the acropolis that Roman influence was most marked. In addition to an Iberian sanctuary there had been a temple 'in antis' of Roman design, if not of Roman workmanship. Here again, above a certain level, adobe material had sufficed. Inside, two bronze heads were found and are identified by some as representations of Augustus and his wife, Livia. If they are, then the cult of Emperor worship can only have been revived in an otherwise deserted town, because, from the evidence of coins and pottery, it is almost certain that Azaila was destroyed during the Sertorian War of the 78-74 B.C. period and never rebuilt. Obvious signs of a desperate defence of the acropolis were seen during the excavations. Stones, for instance, from the sanctuary had been used to make an emergency road-block. It is difficult therefore to envisage circumstances under which the Emperor cult could be expected to flourish here and the problem of the identification of the sculptures remains unsolved.

Leon was built on and over the site of the camp of the VII Legion and the streets of the old part of the town still preserve the outlines of the camp. Considerable portions of the wall still stand at the north end of the camp and thirty-one of the towers out of an estimated total of over seventy. The upper levels date only from the time of Alfonso IX, the lower from the third century, as shown by grave- and altar-stones built into the structure. The gates stood as follow: Puerta del Castillo (north): the south end of the Calle Cardiles (the south, or praetorian gate): Plaza del Obispo (east): Plaza de San Marcelo (west). The walls of Astorga (Asturica Augusta) were also built around the same time and there is the same kind of evidence to suggest this. They were, however, greatly damaged in assaults upon the town in the fighting of 1810.

Coruña has a Roman lighthouse—much reconstructed, of course; the Torre de Hercules, as it is called, has a present height of 185 feet: the original construction of it is attributed to the second century A.D. and was the work of one Gaius Servius Lupus.

It may be that this north-west corner of Spain, owing

to its remoteness, the difficulty of the terrain and the comparative intransigence of its inhabitants, was never provided with a proportionate number of amenities in the way of theatres, circuses, etc., which, in the main, constitute the direct links with Rome that are to be recorded in the rest of the Peninsula. But the Roman baths at Lugo, 95 kms. short of Coruña on the road from Madrid, are proof of the existence of at least some amenities, and at the same time are almost the best specimens of their kind in Spain. Some of the rooms in the building are definitely Roman: their walls of small dressed stones and brick denote a late date: one room, in particular, must have been the 'apodyterium', because a series of niches in the wall complete with semicircular arches are, beyond doubt, the places where the bathers left their clothes.

But the great glory of Lugo is the Roman wall that runs round the town in the rough form of an ellipse with rounded corners. The length of the perimeter falls a few feet short of 7,000, the height varies from 33 to 46 feet, while the width of 20 feet or so has allowed plenty of space for the public to have access to them. As defences for a town, they conform closely to the general specifications laid down by Vitruvius, Augustus's master town-planner: they have thick parapets and semicircular projecting towers at frequent intervals, some few of which have been destroyed. Some sections of the walls have interior galleries and even rooms two or three storeys high, and on the south side, at least one of the towers has what appears to be windows of original date that once served habitations of some sort. Except for the gates and their flanking towers, which are constructed of dressed stonework, the rest is built of slate. In all, they bear a marked resemblance to the walls of Rome that were started by Aurelian and finished by Probus and, in consequence, are supposed to date from the third century. This tentative date is reinforced by the presence in the walls of several tombstones—for it was not uncommon to rob graveyards when large stones were not available—and the years A.D. 250-325 have been suggested as outside limits. The two best-preserved of the Roman gates are in the west wall: they have a semicircular arch at the outer and inner face, connected by vaulting between. The other gates are either reconstructions or modern. These walls at Lugo are the best specimens of their kind in the whole Peninsula and challenge comparison in interest with any others that exist elsewhere.

The last of the major works of the Romans to be mentioned in Tarraconensis, is the tunnel they made through a hill called Montefurado on the southern edge of the modern province of Lugo, when they caused the river Sil to deviate in order to facilitate the extraction of gold from its sands. This tunnel—visible from the railway at one point—is nearly a quarter of a mile long, 50 feet high and nearly 60 wide, and turns very slightly at an angle, about 150 yards from one end.

CHAPTER XII

Lusitania

FOR a short while this, the third and latest of the provincial subdivisions of the Peninsula, included Galicia within its territories, but at a later date, unspecified, save that it was not long delayed, the land north of the Douro was transferred to Tarraconensis. Lusitania, therefore, owing to its comparative remoteness and its restricted area, was always the least populous of the three provinces. Whereas Baetica, comparable in size, had more than one hundred and seventy communities that could be called towns, Lusitania had less than fifty. It must not, however, be supposed from this that the new province created by Augustus languished for any lack of imperial favours: on the contrary, when its capital, Merida, comes under review, it will be seen that its development was pushed ahead with a speed and a lavishness that was, in all probability, quite unique. The site chosen for the capital—within a few miles of the borders of Baetica—is significant of the fact that approach to the province was from the east. Whereas modern Portugal has been drawn to the Atlantic coast by the preponderance of her overseas interests, the reverse was true of the Romans; it is, therefore, not surprising that the majority of the main Roman monuments in Portugal are to be found in the south within measurable distance of the Spanish frontier.

Limited though the geographical area is that comes under review in this chapter, the variety of Roman remains found in the broader acres of Tarraconensis is well maintained. If there is any shift of emphasis, it may be said here to be on bridges, and with the Tagus and the Guadiana, and the Douro and their tributaries impinging upon the province where they do not actually cross it, this can occasion little surprise. The first Roman bridge to be encountered from the north-east is that at Salamanca built over the river Tormes: of its twenty-seven arches, the fifteen that lie nearer to the city retain a good proportion of original Roman stonework, but the other twelve were entirely reconstructed in the year 1677.

About 80 kms. down the modern highway to Merida and Seville, which, in rough outline at least, follows the course of the Roman road that linked the same towns, is the small modern resort of Baños de Montemayor. When the present spa was being built less than 20 yards from the main road through the town the foundations of Roman baths were revealed: altar-stones were also unearthed with dedicatory inscriptions to the nymphs of the spring, made by Roman families who had recovered their health in their waters. These stones are on show to the left of the main entrance hall. Also still preserved is a circular chamber, 26 feet in diameter, with three semicircular niches and in the centre a bath approached by steps.

A little further south is found the now deserted site of Capera, near Oliva, 20 kms. north of Plasencia. The sunken line of an oval rim suggests that the town was important enough to own an amphitheatre, but the main feature of the ruins is an arch of a type unique in Spain, and not commonly found in other parts of the Empire. The arch of Janus at the entrance to the forum boarium in Rome, and that of Marcus Aurelius in Tripoli are two that occur to mind. It has four sides with an archway in each side, and the resultant interior is roofed with a section of groined vaulting. The four pillars on which the arches rest are composed of dressed granite stone. The height of the monument, as it stands today, is nearly 30 feet, and it occupies an area of 27 feet by 23. At each corner stood a column, but none of the four has survived in entirety, and equally unsatisfactory is what is left of the entablature, being a formless mass of concrete that gives no hint of the original design for the top. Roman arches were often crowned by a statue; but in this instance two marble statues of toga-clad persons that were found, belonged to pedestals projecting from the pillars that faced the road which ran through the arch. One of these pedestals bears an inscription that says that the monument was built by Marcus Fidius Macer under directions from the will of his parents.

The little town of Coria (Roman Caurium) which lies west-south-west of Capera, about half the distance to Alcantara near the Portuguese border, retains a considerable proportion of its Roman walls. They have been subjected to demolition and reconstruction in some sections: in others they are lost to view in the houses that have been built on to them. Of the four gates into the town, two are of especial interest, the San Pedro gate and the Puerta del Sol. Both are of the simple type, that is to say, with a single passage way with vaulted roof linking the simple arches that are built, one at each end: both gates are complete with the traditional flanking towers.

Five kilometres south of Plasencia may be seen an

isolated building that has in its day been a hermitage, and incorporated into the western end of it is a structure that was plainly Roman in origin. This section of it looks as though it has been either a small temple or a monumental tomb in temple form, although the existence nearby of a well suggests that it may have been a shrine dedicated to the nymph of some spring. No inscription has ever been found to clarify the matter. The original structure was almost exactly 30 feet square and it rises to a height of about 20 feet. The door in the northern wall is modern, but the one in the east wall is accepted as genuine. There is a peculiar feature on the south wall where in the lower half are eight splayed apertures, in two series of four. The well, that was possibly the inspiration for the building in the first place, is itself surrounded by an old wall 7 feet square and the well and building together bear the significant name of Fuentidueñas.

Some 50 kms. south-west of Plasencia, the modern highway to Caceres crosses the Tagus river, at a point from which can be seen two arches of a ruined bridge some distance upstream. This is all that is left of the once impressive Roman bridge of Alconétar, estimated to have had eighteen arches and to have been 300 yards long. The two major arches that are left, are unusual, being almost flat in design. Significantly they recall the style of bridge which was put over the Danube in Trajan's Dacian Wars: for it is known that one of the first jobs put in hand by Trajan after his accession was the complete overhaul of the road from Astorga to Merida. Several bridges on this Roman road, that have not hitherto been mentioned—including the small bridge over the river Ambroz at Capera—retain varying amounts of original Roman stonework.

The town of Augustobriga (Talavera la Vieja) stood on the west bank of the Tagus, further upstream to the east, not far from the place where the modern highway from Caceres to Madrid crosses it; details of its forum that are given in a publication of the Academy of History are some consolation for the fact that it has not otherwise been preserved. It was 75 yards long in an east-west direction and the plan shows a line of eight columns on the narrow eastern end and one on the south side, relics, presumably, of a portico on these two sides. Northern Europeans need to be reminded that in southern Europe the problem is to get out of the sun, not into it. However, overlooking the river and adjacent to the now non-existent forum, there are the ruins of a structure that is thought to have been a 'curia' or council chamber. There is a base, paved with granite blocks, that with measurements of 22 yards by 13 yards conforms to the standards set by Vitruvius for such buildings: on the side facing the street, where the forum used to be, are four columns with a fifth and sixth behind the two end ones: their bases have ogee mouldings, the pillars are fluted and the capitals are taken to be Corinthian in style. The architrave, now shorn of its stucco, rests upon the capitals: above this, directly over the central pillars that flanked the main entrance, rises a graceful arch of voussoir stones that must originally have been a window to light the interior of the building. This combination of architrave and arch is unique in Roman Spain: the whole is thought to date from around the time of Trajan at the end of the first century A.D.

Also in a position that originally adjoined the forum is a small temple: the platform—again of granite stone—is there, 7 feet high, 27 feet wide and 75 feet long and on the northern edge, the masonry that obviously formed the basis of the steps. Three of the four columns of the façade now incorporated in a later wall are preserved sufficiently to show that their pillars were fluted: the walls of the 'cella' have been rebuilt: through a broken piece of the stairway can be seen the vaulting that supported the floor of the platform. The discovery in the vicinity of an inscribed dedication to Jupiter Optimus Maximus suggests, at least, the probability that this temple was so dedicated.

Near the Portuguese frontier, spanning the Tagus river as part of the road that ran from Caceres to Coimbra, is the Puente de Alcantara, considered by many to be the finest Roman monument in the whole Peninsula. The name Alcantara is due to a Moorish village of that name that was put near the bridge in the later Mohammedan era. The Romans had no settlement in the vicinity. From inscriptions that have survived, it is known that the bridge was built in the year A.D. 106 as a charge upon the eleven towns of the province by Caius Julius Lacer under directions from the Emperor Trajan himself. Built entirely of granite stone, it comprises six arches covering a distance of about 150 yards: the two centre arches are the widest and do not match exactly for size, one measuring just less than 30 yards, the other slightly more: the two smaller arches to the one side are identical in size, not with each other, but with their counterparts on the other side. Since the river here runs in a deep ravine, only the two centre pillars stand in water, but all five pillars are built in two sections, the lower sections projecting upstream to a point, downstream to a square end. The difference of height between the pillars is taken up in the heavier, lower sections and as the six

L

arches spring from about the same level on their pillars, a pleasing and artistic effect is achieved. Including the approaches, the entire bridge is 210 yards, 26 feet wide and at its highest point over 150 feet high. During the course of its long history it has suffered varying degrees of damage and it was last restored in 1860, but it remains in all essentials a Roman bridge.

Two adjuncts to the bridge remain to be described. Spanning the roadway, directly above the centre pillar stands an arch erected in honour of Trajan, as is made clear by an inscription on the entablature. It has suffered on at least two occasions from indiscreet restoration, represented by the false battlement that crowns it and by the more obvious addition of the crests of Charles V and Isabel II. At the head of the bridge is a small stone-built temple complete with pointed roof whose interior measures 17 feet long by 13 feet wide by 21 feet high. A stairway leads up to the doorway, which has a Tuscan column at each side: the only other decoration that the façade possesses is a rather heavy moulding on the cornice and round the pediment. Above the door, occupying the full space of the entablature is a marble stone bearing an inscription put there in 1648 to perpetuate the original dedication of the temple to Trajan and mentioning the architect of both bridge and temple to be Gaius Julius Lacer. Even so, some authorities have made bold to suggest that the temple was really the mausoleum of the architect, appropriately set to overlook his finest monument.

It may not, however, have been his only monument in that part of the world: for there is a second Roman bridge over the river Elja, a few kilometres further on where the old Roman road meets the modern frontier with Portugal. It is 90 yards long and has five arches, the centre one being the longest: the whole is in a good state of preservation.

Caceres, Colonia Norba of the Romans, can boast of no major monument of the Romans, but the Casa de las Veletas in the Plaza of the same name, houses a good selection of smaller finds: among these was the pedestal of a silver statue, that, according to the inscription on it, was raised to the honour of the Emperor Severus by order of the town council of Norba. Severus died in York in A.D. 211. The medieval walls of the city, too, preserve the line of the original Roman defences: for in many places they retain Roman work in them, particularly in the arch of the Puerta del Cristo in the south wall. Interest, however, can be maintained beyond the walls, because one of the two camps that Metellus made in the neighbourhood, in his attempts to cope with the guerrilla tactics of Sertorius in the year 79 B.C., has been identified at Caceres el Viejo, 2 kms. north-east of the city: it was set on a small hill and clearly discernible outlines reveal the plan of the walls, which were nearly 7 feet thick, and the position of the gates. The plan was a perfect rectangle of 700 yards by 400 yards. Almost a dozen tall, bomb-like amphorae, found within the precincts of the camp, are now housed in the above-mentioned Casa de las Veletas.

The provincial capital is metaphorically, so to speak, just over the southern horizon, but whereas the proximity of Merida may dwarf the ruins of Colonia Metellinensis, it should not deny them a brief mention. They are to be seen on the southern slope of the hill whereon now stands the medieval castle of Medellin, a few miles upstream on the banks of the Guadiana river. Chief among them were remnants of a wall that was once thought to be part of a town wall, but, recently has been shown to be the outer semicircular wall of a small theatre. Further investigation soon brought to light unmistakable evidence of a concentric vaulted gallery that provided entrances to and exits from the centre block of seats: the lowest range of seats still lies below ground-level. The church of Santiago has been built over the stage, but the top of an arch can be seen below the wall of the sacristy.

Most of the cities of Spain that owe their origin to Rome—Seville, Cordoba, Barcelona, Saragossa are examples—under later civilisations grew to a greatness that their founders can never have foreseen and in the process virtually obliterated their Roman connections, acquiring in exchange medieval treasures of church and palace that ensure their place high in the list of Europe's historic cities. Even Tarragona, which has not grown noticeably in size, is crowned with a fifteenth-century Cathedral that many connoisseurs hold to be the most beautiful in Spain. But Merida, standing, a little forlornly, on a low hill by the Guadiana, overlooking the Estremaduran plain, has an air of a town that time has passed by, offering but scant recompense for departed glories. Chosen by Augustus and his advisers in 25 B.C. to be the capital of a new Spanish province, it was a site that never again found marked favour with later generations of invaders. So the interest of Merida is still almost entirely Roman, with little else overlaid, and since few towns in the Roman Empire exhibit so many Roman remains, pride of place within the pages of this book cannot rightly be withheld.

The town began life as a small Celtic settlement of

unknown title. A slight hill, an island in the river to make the crossing easier were a combination that often proved decisive in the location of early settlements. Rome itself started from just such a combination. However, when the new town came to be constructed, access to it from the south was the first need. Hence the long, low bridge over the Guadiana is its oldest monument. What impresses at first sight is the apparently needless length of it—nearly half a mile: for of the sixty arches, fewer than half normally have contact with the water —the rest carrying the road on an embankment over the low ground to the south of the river, or spanning the island that divides the river bed at this point. But a brief inspection reveals that the bridge has three distinct sections. The first spans that part of the river between the town and the island and rises slightly towards the centre from each side. These eight arches —each almost 23 feet wide—spring from pillars that are themselves pierced by smaller flood-arches and rest upon bases that are rounded to meet the flow of the water. The roadway, about 20 feet wide, is laid only two thin courses above the upper limits of the arches. A ramp leads down from the south side of the bridge on to the island which was once the terminus of the river traffic and where the evidence of a wharf and of either warehouses or shops has been found. The second section spans the swifter-flowing half of the river and it, too, rises gently towards the centre. The third section at the end is mounted on twenty-one close-set piers that are not provided with flood-arches. The whole bridge is built of dressed stone and very many of the pieces retain the holes that were put in them to enable them to be set in position by crane. The style of work is not uniform throughout the full length because from time to time some measure of restoration has proved necessary: there is literary evidence for at least four occasions, in 686 under the Visigoth King Ervigius, in 1610, and twice in the nineteenth century, 1823 and 1879.

The length of the bridge is at once both an indication of the proportions that a flood could assume and a tribute to the thoroughness of the Romans in their plans. If the latter required any confirmation, the stone embankment that was built along the riverside to protect the town, would provide it. Starting from the bridge it runs upstream for just on 400 yards and consists of sixty-four bays, each marked by an external buttress, the whole composed of substantial stone blocks. Here, too, is the first evidence of the extensive sewage system that the Romans provided for the town. Fourteen sewers running from east to west have been identified, with nine others crossing them at right angles: of the fourteen six emerge in the stone embankment, at buttress numbers, 1, 14, 21, 35, 54, 63. With the exception of the first-mentioned, the openings are rectangular 4 feet high and nearly 2 feet wide: these dimensions are retained for the actual sewers within, save that the roof is arched in tiles and it is the continuation of the arched roof to the actual entrance that distinguishes the first opening from the others. All the openings were barred by iron gratings that were set in lead, the holes for which are still visible in the stonework today. The floors are of cement, and the walls of stone, and the likelihood that the whole sewage system dates from very early in the town's development is made a virtual certainty by the discovery of a section of it under the theatre which was built in A.D. 18.

The road to the north was next secured by the

building of the bridge over the Rio Albarregas. It is, of course, much smaller than the Guadiana bridge, having only four arches with two flood gaps in the embankment that leads on to it. Even the stones used were smaller, and being badly weathered, do not show so many shear holes for craning. The parapet is not original work.

At one time it was thought that the first defensive walls enclosed a very restricted area between the Guadiana bridge and the arch of Trajan in the centre of the town, which was mistakenly accepted as having been a gate in a wall. But investigations have shown that the allegedly later wall was already in existence when the amphitheatre was built in 8 B.C. and preceded the Cornalvo aqueduct also, which was of even earlier date; consequently the idea of an inner, shorter wall has been rejected.

The two traditional main streets of a Roman town, crossing at right angles, as in a military camp, are there to be seen in Merida: the Calle de Santa Eulalia that leads directly eastwards from the main river bridge and its counterpart, not now so well defined, that begins at the bridge over the Albarregas and passing under the Arch of Trajan ends in the southern section of the town. The ends of these two main arteries must have been marked by gates in the city walls: in fact, the site of the one near the Guadiana bridge was found to have been used later for the same purpose by both the Visigoths and the Arabs: at the other end of the same street, the foundations of the gate were found beneath the pavement at a place that is still called Puerta de la Villa. There was at least one more gate, to give access to the theatre and the amphitheatre, and possibly posterns in addition, leading from the

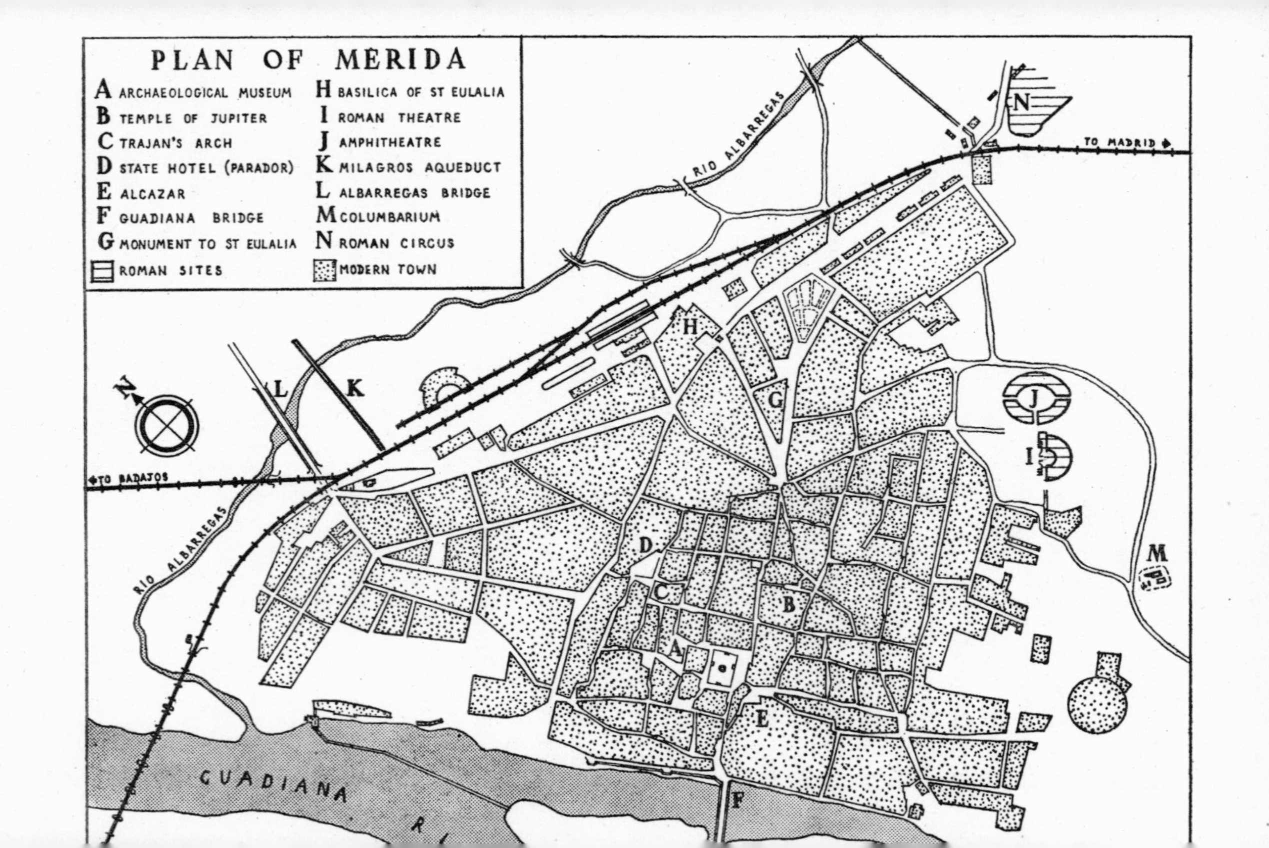
PLAN OF MERIDA
A ARCHAEOLOGICAL MUSEUM
B TEMPLE OF JUPITER
C TRAJAN'S ARCH
D STATE HOTEL (PARADOR)
E ALCAZAR
F GUADIANA BRIDGE
G MONUMENT TO ST EULALIA
ROMAN SITES
H BASILICA OF ST EULALIA
I ROMAN THEATRE
J AMPHITHEATRE
K MILAGROS AQUEDUCT
L ALBARREGAS BRIDGE
M COLUMBARIUM
N ROMAN CIRCUS
MODERN TOWN
TO MADRID
TO BADAJOS
RIO ALBARREGAS
RIO ALBARREGAS
GUADIANA
N

embankment on the river side. The present coat of arms of Merida consists of a representation of one of its own Roman gateways as depicted on coins that were minted in the town under sanction from Augustus. At the time of its erection, the wall was obviously intended to be a normal, defensive wall—for where it is visible today, near the amphitheatre, it is 9 feet thick: but later, as the country proved to be so peaceable and free from invasions, breaches in them, in the form of posterns, could have been permitted without any loss of security.

It is now time to take up the tale of the three aqueducts, one after the other. It is very likely that the theatre was built in the period that separates the second aqueduct from the first: but since the theatre has been fully described in an earlier chapter, the three aqueducts may be taken together. The earliest aqueduct is undoubtedly the Cornalvo—that of which the least evidence has survived, mainly because it followed the contours of the countryside on its way from the reservoir of the same name that lies 15 kms. to the east of the town, and in no part required any higher superstructure than a solid wall could provide. It is part of this solid wall that can still be found, closely adjacent to the line of the city wall, between the Roman theatre and the modern bull-ring to the south-east of the town. The channel of this aqueduct is larger than that of either of the other two and is introduced into the town at a point where its waters can be most effectively distributed, and it is on these two factors that its claim to be considered the oldest mainly rests.

If the Guadiana was rejected as an unsuitable source for the town's water supply, it would soon become apparent that more water must be laid on to combat the fierce summers of Estremadura, and there are certain similarities in the brickwork of the later aqueducts and in that of the amphitheatre, that have led experts to conclude that they all date from round about the same time—8 B.C. Of the two aqueducts, the Los Milagros has arches that are less skilfully tiled than those of San Lazaros and may therefore be assumed to have been the earlier of the two. The very considerable remains of it cross the Albarregas valley to the north of the town, parallel to and to the east of the road bridge that has already been mentioned, and extend over a distance of more than half a mile. Thirty-eight pillars still stand, many of them linked by the topmost of the three connecting arches they once possessed. The maximum height they attain slightly exceeds 80 feet, and they have for hundreds of years now proved acceptable nesting-places for storks. Their ruined condition makes it easy to observe the method of their construction. The pillars, 9 feet square, were built round a concrete core: the outer covering was of stone and brick, five layers of each alternating to give a pleasing artistic effect. The bricks act as a bonding course right through the structure, but even with a projecting buttress on each of the two outer sides, the result does not inspire confidence by modern standards of building or even by later ones of the Romans' own. The excellence of the mortar used must have contributed largely to the survival of what is left today. The same fundamental weakness may be noted in the third and last of the aqueducts, the San Lazaros, whose scanty remains are visible on the left where the Toledo road leaves the railway and the town.

Nothing illustrates better the care and forethought with which this town was founded than the creation of two reservoirs to store the water that served the first two of the aqueducts. The Cornalvo reservoir lies 15 kms. to the east. Two miles long, it is divided at one point by an artificial embankment, 250 yards long and nearly 20 yards high. On the bank stands a solidly built, granite stone tower, some 14 feet square with a square aperture in the south wall. Inside the building, some 50 feet below ground-level, a vaulted passage leads off beneath the reservoir in one direction and under the embankment in the other.

The reservoir of Proserpina that supplied water along the Los Milagros aqueduct is about 3 miles north of the town: its name is due to no other circumstance than the chance discovery in the neighbourhood of a dedicatory inscription to the goddess. Smaller than the Cornalvo reservoir, having a perimeter of about 3 miles only, the Proserpina forms a natural ellipse whose north-western end is cut short by a retaining wall, a quarter of a mile long, that forms a slight angle to meet the thrust of the water. Two square towers provide access in their interior to the pipes through which the water passed.

The elaborate provision of artificial supplies of water did not mean, however, that the Guadiana was entirely neglected. Underneath the Alcazar, the Moorish fortification that commands the entrance to the bridge from the town, is a large water tank, 23 feet by 12 feet, that is obviously the work of Roman masons. The tank is divided into two sections, the second acting as an overflow to the first, which draws its supply directly from the river. The whole chamber is covered with a vaulted roof of exceptional beauty. Similar arrangements for water storage were found under the ground-level of several houses in Merida, set beneath the patio to receive any rain that might fall into it.

The amphitheatre which adjoins the theatre on the south-eastern edge of the town confirms the development in the use of building materials that has already been noted in the description of the two later aqueducts —namely, the increasing use of tiles or bricks. For instance, there is much more tile-facing in the amphitheatre than in the theatre: in the former the whole of the front wall that supports the second tier of seats is tile-faced and the tiles used are of exactly the same dimensions as those employed in the construction of the Los Milagros and San Lazaros aqueducts. But where arches had to carry any considerable weight, stone is exclusively used and the piers are often arranged in the 'long and short' work which the Saxons in England appear to have copied. This arrangement of headers and stretchers enabled a better bonding to be made with the adjoining material: it was first noticed in this book in the Temple of Vich in Catalonia. Architecturally all the buildings at Merida so far mentioned are worthy of the close attention of specialists because they represent first-class specimens of early Augustan building in a part of the Empire where new styles were free to be developed, unhampered by the conservatism that shrouded contemporary work in Rome.

The amphitheatre at Merida never had the towering façade of a colosseum, for it was dug deep down into a hillside: and it was not so large as the one at Italica near Seville, measuring only 137 yards by 110 yards. Nevertheless, it is calculated to have been capable of seating 15,000. Of the three tiers of seats, the lowest tier of ten rows is clearly visible: in one section of them, seven rows still retain their stone dressing: in another, some rather clumsy restoration has been done; in front, bordering the edge of the arena, is the 5-foot space for the chairs of the magistrates and visiting dignitaries. The middle tier contained eleven rows and they become increasingly difficult to identify; and eleven as the number of the third and top tier of seats is a mere conjecture arrived at by a careful study of the broken remains that lie fallen on the ground.

Contrary to the usual practice in such buildings, there are no underground concentric galleries, linking the 'vomitoria' or exits. Here the exits in the face of the auditorium communicate directly with the exterior by means of radial passages, in which, to right and left, can be seen the lower ranges of stone stairways that used to lead to the higher tiers. The pathway behind the first series of seats is reached by a descending stairway, and is not served directly by a 'vomitorium'.

There are three gateways that lead to the arena: those at the north and south ends descend so steeply that it seems likely that they, too, were stairways. Immediately to right and left were the premises where the gladiators and prisoners who were condemned to take part in the proceedings, were temporarily housed. There was a door that led into each of these rooms from the gateway and another that opened directly on to the arena. Needless to say, these doors would be carefully barred and holes have been found in the sides into which an iron grating was possibly once fixed. But the main entrance into the arena is in the centre of the west side and over the actual point of entrance was erected the tribune for the presiding magistrate with steps leading up to it on both sides of the passageway. Directly opposite, across the shorter axis of the arena, a gap in the lowest rows of seats indicates the site of the tribune reserved for the person who presented the games: beneath was a small brick-walled rest room with a hint of plastering that suggested a mural painting.

The section of the arena that had premises beneath it, is very clearly indicated: stretching down the line of the longer axis, it forms one large rectangle with smaller rectangular projections towards the north and south entrances. Beneath these were found five parallel passages, the centre one the deepest. The one to either side of the centre had rough ramps and was probably used to get animals up into the arena. The quadrilateral centre piece with which the passages communicate, is connected with a drain which, passing under the western half of the auditorium and the rear premises of the theatre, joins the main sewage system of the town. At its lowest level, under the centre, the underground chamber was 16 feet deep.

The date of the completion of the whole amphitheatre was decisively fixed by the discovery of two inscriptions on granite blocks that had fallen from the front of the two tribunals of honour. By a precise reference to the number of times that Augustus had held his tribunician powers, the year 8 B.C. is indicated.

Although from the evidence of the use made of the building materials it is evidently early Augustan work, no such exact date can be given to the circus that lies a quarter of a mile to the east of the old walls, just beyond the point where the road and railway to Madrid cross each other. It lies on an east-west axis, 470 yards long and 120 yards wide. The spectators sat on seven rows of seats that were ranged round the semicircular end and the two long sides, and there would be room for nearly thirty thousand of them. On the north side the seating was supported by vaulted arches: on the south side the three rows of front seats can be identified: behind them, parallel walls that supported the four back rows of seats which may have been of wood.

The spina, or central ridge, is there, 1 yard high, running for 250 yards—in two sections of unequal length—down the centre of the arena on the usual, slightly oblique line. On the top, at various intervals are gaps that once held the bases of obelisks and statues. At the western end the exact site of the seven starting gates or pens (carceres) were unearthed, each almost 12 feet wide, just sufficient to take a four-horse team.

It was near these 'carceres' that an inscription dating from between A.D. 337 and A.D. 340 was found. In graceful words, typical of the age, it speaks of the restoration of the circus undertaken at that time: interesting reference is also given to arrangements made to flood the circus ('aquis inundari') for the purpose of staging a mock sea battle. This must have entailed piping water from the nearby aqueduct of San Lazaro.

This is the last of the circuses to be noted in Spain, but, combined with those discovered—and previously mentioned—at Tarragona, Saguntum, Calahorra and Toledo, it makes an impressive list that speaks of considerable enthusiasm inside the country for the sport of racing. But this is not surprising when it is remembered that Asturian horses, in particular, were renowned throughout the Empire for their speed.

So far the Roman structures that have come under review, including the casa Romana-basilica that was described in a previous chapter in connection with early Christianity, are found on the outer perimeter of the town or beyond. Yet the town itself was well stocked with Roman buildings, many of which have survived to the present day in varying degrees of completeness and after suffering varying degrees of adaptation and mal-treatment. The first temple that can be mentioned provides a fair example of the vicissitudes they underwent.

A temple that, without any known good reason, bears the title of Diana is to be found in a prominent position in the town on the Calle de Santa Catalina. Despite the fact that it suffered the indignity of having the Palace of the Conde de los Corbos built on it in the sixteenth century, it is still easily recognisable as a normal Roman temple, hexastyle and peripteral. The six columns along the front were matched by nine down each side: seventeen of these survive, some without capitals, but all of the Corinthian order with fluted pillars: they rise to a height of some 26 feet above the platform on which the temple stood. The best preserved are the five complete columns that face the west, four of which support their section of the architrave. Details of the 'cella' are lost beneath the intruding sixteenth-century 'Casona' or palace.

Close by the Church of Santa Eulalia, not far from the modern railway station, is a small chapel similarly dedicated to the young girl who was sanctified for the martyrdom by burning that she suffered on this very spot. The small porch that stands before its entrance comprises all that is left of the one-time temple of Mars: two columns with two square 'antae' between them support an architrave and frieze, while behind, against the wall of the chapel, with the door between them, are set two more 'antae', supporting the rear of the porch. Obviously, the temple of Mars had been a 'templum in antis', i.e. the side walls of the cella projected forward, and a glance at the two columns reveals equally obviously that it was of the Corinthian order. The pillars of the columns are smooth monoliths and have been cut short to serve their purpose

Merida. Amphitheatre—entrance to gladiators' quarters; note ventilation shaft on left

Merida. Theatre—entrance to central block of seats

Merida

Above. Bridge over the Guadiana

Left. Masonry wall on Guadiana showing outlet of sewer

here. The architrave has fine mouldings running the length of it and among the ornate carvings of the surmounting frieze are several heads of Medusa. This ornamentation, however, is interrupted in the centre to make room for four words of Latin inscription that tell us that the temple was dedicated to Mars by Vettilla, wife of Paculus. Mars was associated with agriculture as well as war and his sanctuaries were often extra-mural, as this presumably was. It is surmised, therefore, that Paculus was a landowning farmer of the town, and that this small temple was raised in his honour: the remnants of it were built into the present structure in 1617, but experts have deduced from the style of the inscription that they dated originally from about Nero's time, in the middle of the first century A.D.

In the Plaza de Santiago is a building that was once the convent de Jesus which has marble pillars from a Roman temple incorporated into its cloister: these were found lying among the foundations of a Roman temple when the convent was built in 1646 and they had obviously served an alien purpose before in some mosque, for prayers in Arabic script were found superficially scratched on their surface. But the most interesting find was a pedestal of red marble with the words CONCORDIAE AUGUSTI carved in a style that suggests the second century A.D. as their date of origin. Doubtless, therefore, the temple was dedicated to the cult of successively deified emperors. Altar-stones from this same site, decorated with carvings of garlands and instruments of sacrifice, were used to make the column that was raised in honour of Santa Eulalia in the gardens of the Ramblas of the same name.

A temple of triple dedication to Jupiter and Juno

and Minerva is thought once to have stood where the Calle de Baños and Sagasta meet near the centre of the town. Present evidence is unconvincing: for it amounts to no more than a section of concrete stairway in the patio of the house that stands on the corner of the two streets. Fortunately, when the Conte de Laborde was making his tour of Spain in the early nineteenth century, there was sufficient material to devise a plan of the whole. If we accept his plan, therefore, it was an octostyle temple—twenty-eight columns in all. The cella was divided into three parts, nave and two aisles, by two rows of up to nine columns. The nave had an apsidal end, the aisles ended in small, square projections. A section of cornice, two Corinthian capitals, two fine statues—one of Marcus Agrippa and another of an unidentified, toga-clad person—were found on the site and may be seen in the Archaeological Museum near the Plaza Mayor. The workmanship revealed in these pieces is up to the best of Augustan standards, as they would be expected to be, if the surmise about the dedication of the building be correct: for there was an element of State religion in this triple dedication, and any temple so dedicated would be among the first to be built. But if de Laborde's plan of construction is rejected, a good case can be made for its having been a basilica or a curia. Incidentally, in 1929 there was unearthed from in front of it a magnificent keystone representing the head and shoulders of a bull. It is one of Spain's finest pieces of Roman sculpture and is housed in the local Archaeological Museum.

The last of Merida's temples to be reviewed strikes a familiar note to anyone who remembers his London of 1954: for it repeats the combination of the Persian

Mithras and the Egyptian Serapis, whose temple, when discovered in the City during the autumn of that year, proved a nine days' wonder. Such temples were commonly placed on the fringe of communities, and Merida was no exception in this. It was during the excavations involved in the construction of the modern bull-ring on the edge of the town that the sanctuary came to light. Unfortunately, no architectural details have survived—only debris, which carried evidence of mural painting and dedicatory altars that put the identification of the temple beyond doubt: among the plethora of marble statuary that was also found was a fine head of Serapis and representations of Mithras and his lion-headed attendants, of Oceanus, and Mercury, Venus and Aesculapius.

The so-called Arch of Trajan spans a street near the Plaza de Santiago. The sides are built into the walls of adjoining houses, and inside one of them can be seen the bonding courses that linked the arch to a now non-existent wall. The single arch spans an area of more than 26 feet across and 16 feet deep. Lacking architrave and entablature, the single line of giant granite voussoirs stand out starkly against the sky: for, when complete, the whole probably attained a height of almost 60 feet. But the dimensions of the arch are more easily determined than its purpose. The idea that it was ever the north gate of an earlier and smaller set of defensive walls can fairly safely be rejected, because the allegedly later walls are themselves so early in date, and come so soon after the known date of the town's foundation as to render unlikely any predecessors: and in any case, the general appearance of the arch is alien to any suggestion of defence. On the other hand, the site it occupied in relation to the plan of the Roman town was an excellent one for a free-standing arch.

Contrary to the usual practice of the Romans, the baths at Merida were not found in the suburbs, but to the east, on high ground facing the town. The main feature was a circular chamber, some 20 feet in diameter, with brick walls and a hint of vaulting still left: from it led off a small blackened chamber and two galleries, the narrower of which ended in a room 13 feet by 16, counting an apse. This may possibly have been the 'laconium', the equivalent of the Turkish bath. A further passage from here led steeply down to a well. Further evidence of baths has also been found; to the north-east of the town a frigidarium with a drain leading from the actual bath and the outlines of more than one circular room; to the south, a hypocaust with brick pillars just over 1 yard high to support the floor above.

Finally, in this survey of Roman Merida—burials. True to tradition, these are to be sought adjoining the main highways leading out of the town, and indeed one area has been located on each side of the road to Seville, beyond the Guadiana bridge. But, of greater interest, because they have been more extensively excavated, are two family vaults that were found facing each other, just outside the line of the old city wall to the south-west of the Roman theatre. Square and rectangular respectively, they are stone-built and their interiors were originally finished in plaster. The tops of the walls were rounded and it is clear that they were never roofed in. The name of the family concerned is inscribed above the doorway in each building. The square one belonged to the Volconii and in the niches made in the lower half of the far and side walls rested the ashes of four persons, together with details of identification: to the right of the door a mother; on the far wall a brother and sister; to the left a man who was probably master of the house in his day: in the centre of the floor is a square block of masonry to serve, possibly, as a table at the funeral feast. The other was owned by a family of Julii who enjoyed full Roman citizenship: six urns were found in this one: adjoining is an erection, triangular in shape, that may have served as an 'ustrinum' or crematorium.

Before moving west to complete the survey of Roman Portugal, the baths at Alange (Castrum Colubri) south-east of Merida claim attention: for two of the rooms in the existing establishment are genuinely Roman, and, being alike, are thought to have been 'frigidaria', one for each sex. The original door in each can be seen to have been blocked up and the present two substituted in comparatively recent times. Both rooms are circular and covered by a semicircular cupola: in the wall of each are four equally spaced niches. The circular baths have three rows of steps that lead down into them, and the sections of these that are original still retain their marble. The 16 feet diameter of the actual bath compares with 36 feet for the whole room. Whitewash now adorns the walls, in all probability, once decked with mural paintings, and mosaics have given place to tiles on the floor: but lead pipes still serve to lay the water on and drain it away. A single altar stone was found on the site, dedicated to Juno, Queen of Heaven, by parents in gratitude for their son's recovery of health in these waters.

The road system of that part of Portugal, south of the Douro river, which was in the province of Lusitania and to which we must now turn, was linked to the important north-south highway from Astorga to Seville via Salamanca, Caceres and Merida. Branch roads leading west, left it at three main places: from Caceres north-west to the Douro: from Merida to Lisbon (Olisipo) by two routes; the northerly one via Santarem (Scallabis) and the right bank of the Tagus; the lower one by Evora, Alcacer do Sal (Salacia) to a point on the river opposite Lisbon; from Seville to Beja (Pax Julia) and to Alcacer do Sal with a branch road from Castro Marim (Baesuris) along the south coast to Faro (Ossonoba) and Lagos. From Lisbon upwards the western ends of these main roads and their subsidiaries were sealed off, so to speak, by a road that ran from Lisbon through Santarem and Coimbra (Aeminium) to the mouth of the Douro and beyond to Braga.

In the nature of things, owing to its remoteness and the comparatively small population of those days, Portugal could not be expected to produce any large number of major relics, and there are, in fact, only two centres—Conimbriga, south of Coimbra, and Evora—that can claim attention for major exhibits. But it would be a mistake to assume that this part of the Peninsula has been neglected archaeologically: on the contrary, under the impulse of separate nationalistic feeling, much excellent work has been done and provincial museums have an abundance of smaller Roman finds to show, and where, as at Conimbriga, there is scope for a major display, it is carried out with a neatness and efficiency that we associate with the work of our own Ministry of Works on the sites of medieval monasteries.

Conimbriga was a Lusitanian settlement, typically set in a naturally strong position, on a rocky promontory dominating two deep valleys. It was selected deliberately by the Romans as a centre to be developed for the dissemination of the Roman way of life, in the territory that lies between the Tagus and the Douro. The walls enclose a triangular piece of land at the tip of the promontory: the north and south walls that lead out from the apex are each about a quarter of a mile long and their course is directed by limits of the level land available, and with a height of more than 20 feet and a thickness of up to 14 feet, they form a very formidable defence. The east wall of about 200 yards has no such naturally defensive qualities and in order to make the best use of the terrain a considerable part of the city was left outside the walls. Since the part thus excluded was the richest and most prosperous of the whole town, it would be reasonable to assign a late date for their construction, perhaps in the third or fourth century when barbaric invasions from the east were beginning to reach the Peninsula. In the walls themselves there is evidence of hurried construction. Votive tablets and tombstones have been found in the walls of the other towns—Lugo and Leon, to name only two, but here they have been found in such profusion, along with statues even, as to suggest not only a hint of panic, but also a complete disregard for pagan religion.

It was in the vicinity of the east wall that extensive excavations were made in the year 1938. By the nature of the site, gates to the town were restricted to this wall: they are two in number and the main one, the Puerta de Tomar, is the lower of the two. It was built of solid masonry and involved a covered passageway some 25 feet long between two squat towers. An aqueduct of earlier date than the walls entered the town just below the second and smaller gate, bringing an abundant supply of water from the spring of Alca-bideque: appropriate buildings had been erected in the neighbourhood: one that was propped against the north side of the aqueduct inside the wall contained two baths (piscinae) close to a separate structure with a central corridor flanked by four apsidal chambers built over hypocausts to provide hot baths. To the south of the aqueduct was a house of two storeys, used either for trade or possibly as an inn: inside was a patio with some provision for water storage beneath.

In 1938, under Government sponsorship, a new road was built to provide easier access to the site for tourists and it was when the end of this new road was being made just outside the Puerta de Tomar that the foundations of a larger house or minor palace were brought to light. It stood hard up against the town wall, immediately to the right of the gate and the road, on a terrace partly natural, partly artificial, overlooking the stream which passes under the aqueduct. The total frontage facing the road and almost at right angles to the gate, was more than 160 feet long. Access to the vestibule was across a portico and beyond to the inner courtyard, by a double set of doors. This courtyard, with the main rooms beyond, was the chief feature of the building, containing no less than twenty-six columns round an elaborate set-piece, a rectangular block of stone carved into a bold pattern and inset below ground-level. The quarters to the right of this main 'patio' were built round a small patio of their own and were, in all probability, for the servants. On the far side, two flights of stairs lead down to the latrines, through which the 'impluvia' above could be drained. A feature of this house, and indeed of the whole town so far as it has been excavated, is the lavish amount of water that was laid on. The explanation is not far to seek, when it is remembered that this part of the Peninsula is subject to an Atlantic rather than a Mediterranean climate.

This fine specimen of domestic architecture of the late Empire remarkable for its originality in boldly adapting traditional design to the site on which it was built, is not unique even in Conimbriga. A similar construction was brought to light, this time inside the main gateway (Puerta de Tomar) immediately to the left and adjoining the wall. The main patio here is squarer than its counterpart outside the gate, but twenty-four columns stand round a similarly elaborate impluvium. Incorporated into the rear premises, however, is a complete bathing establishment. A water conduit passed under the house and would not be noteworthy in itself were it not for a 'lanterna', a round aperture fitted with a stone grid of six propeller-like shafts radiating from the centre: this lies in front of the house and may have been a means of draining the street.

Naturally, where so markedly a residential district has been the subject of excavation, the yield of mosaics and *objets d'art* is correspondingly large. The tessellated floors, in particular, are numerous and of exceptional quality: conspicuous among the rest are a small bronze statue of Minerva, the head of an unknown woman carved in marble, and a stone lion that was used in the building of the walls. Such pieces as are not exhibited at the site are to be seen in the Museu de Marchado in Coimbra.

The Roman town of Olisipo has suffered the fate of most places that have later become national capitals. Virtually all traces of the original settlement, on the hill where the Chateau stands, have been obliterated. In 1798, however, a Roman theatre was discovered near the Chateau with evidence to show that it was built in A.D. 57. Only two statues survived, one a representation of Silenus in a state of intoxication. Vestiges of two bathing establishments are also to be seen, the Thermae Cassiorum near Pedras Negras and, in the Rua da Prata, the second, associated with a sanctuary to Aesculapius, the god of healing. A stone inscribed in memory of a certain L. Lucretius was unearthed near the Cathedral and is now in the Museu do Carmo.

Santarem, 78 kms. further up the Tagus, has nothing Roman to show, although, as Scallabis, it was the capital of a subdivision (conventus) of the province. Further east, near the Spanish frontier, Portalegre (Amoia) and Aramenha (Medobriga) 12 kms. away are more promising and would repay investigation by experts. Already in the district is to be seen the best-preserved Roman bridge in Portugal at Vila Formosa between Alter do Chão and the village of Seda to the west. It was part of the military road from Merida to Lisbon. While not so large as the bridge over the Guadiana at Merida—having only six arches and being only 127 yards long—none the less it bears a striking resemblance to it in the type of stone used and particularly in having the same kind of flood-arches, although in this case they are found level with the top half of the main arches and not in the actual pillars of the bridge. The height of the bridge is 25 feet and the width of it 22 feet.

On a sandy spit of land that juts out into the estuary opposite Setubal, below Lisbon, was a Roman settlement called Troia. At low tide remnants of houses protrude from the sand. Limited discoveries have been made here: baths, in a private house, with a tessellated floor, and a carved stone panel representing Mithras. Attended by a snake and other symbols, he stands by a table of ritual feasting, his head surrounded by a halo of radiant light.

In so far as the landscape of the whole Peninsula is harsher and more forbidding than the lush, green countryside of England, there would be less inclination to build out in the country the villas that were so conspicuous a feature of the later centuries of the Roman occupation of Britain: and in any event there is not the slightest evidence that the policy of urbanisation which was officially modified or even, eventually, abandoned in Britain, ever suffered a similar fate in the Spanish provinces. But that is not to deny the existence of country villas there: some have already been noted on the coast near Valencia: and a particularly sumptuous one has been found in a village between Estremoz and Evora Monte, not far south of the modern Badajoz-Lisbon highway: another, the Villa de Torre de Palma, about 35 kms. to the north-east near Monforte. Both were possessed of exceptional mosaics that are now exhibited in the Ethnological Museum in Belem, a suburb of Lisbon: from the former, representations of Ulysses in his boat, listening to the sirens, and of a slave being chastised: from the latter, the owners' favourite horses and their names, the Muses, the cortège of Bacchus and Theseus killing the Minotaur.

Late in the period of Roman rule, as a natural consequence of declining interest in urban life which was becoming more and more stereotyped, some country houses were so far extended as to cover as much acreage as a medieval monastery. The Villa Fortunatus at Fraga has already been mentioned: others have been found at Clunia, Cuevas de Soria, near Tarragona (Selva del Camp), near Leon (Santa Colomba de Somoza), near Valladolid (Almenara de Adaja) and as far away as Navarre (Liédena). But the largest of all, the Villa de la Cocosa, was discovered 17 kms. south of Badajoz about twelve years ago when the quest for local building stone unearthed a section of Roman mosaic. Subsequent official excavations uncovered a rambling block of buildings incorporating the best part of a hundred rooms.

The main rooms grouped round the large atrium or peristyle were not conspicuous for their sumptuousness, and mosaic floors were few. The other rooms, mainly to the north-west and east of the peristyle included the full range of baths, served by a private aqueduct and two sections, dedicated for Christian use, with a third, a quatrefoil chapel and baptisterium in the Byzantine style, 250 yards to the south-east. Let it be said immediately that experts have decided that none of the Christian sections dates from earlier than the Visigothic period, to which also are assigned two similar Christian chapels, the Casa Herrera, 4 kms. north of Merida, and the Vega del Mar, near Malaga. The mosaics belonged to the second century A.D., and the villa is thought to have been started even earlier, possibly in the middle of the first century A.D. Coins have been found on the site ranging from Agrippa, cofounder of Merida, to Arcadius, early in the fifth century. Unlike the Villa Fortunatus at Fraga, this estate appears to have survived the Germanic invasions unscathed, but the absence of any sort of Moorish coinage suggests that it suffered the common fate of many Christian centres in the eighth century.

Evora, today no longer on the main road from Merida to Lisbon, but on a loop-road that is dependent from it, first claimed historical attention as the headquarters of Sertorius before his military successes allowed him to transfer to Huesca in the foothills of the Pyrenees. Secluded among the many architectural treasures of the sixteenth and seventeenth centuries, for which the town is famous, a few relics of Rome may still be seen: many others provided raw material for the above-mentioned treasures. Only one of the early gates of the town has survived with any elements of Roman work in it, the Arco de D. Isabel: and it is known that a Roman triumphal or commemorative arch was demolished in 1570 and the marble from it used in the construction of the Jesuit college. The Archaeological Museum on the ground floor of the Public Library has much of interest to show in the range of smaller Roman pieces. Larger items have been transferred elsewhere: for instance, of two sarcophagi found in the neighbourhood, one with elaborate carvings of lions' heads is housed at Belem, the other of solid marble, with the four sides bearing carved representations of the four seasons, has been transported to far-away Oporto and rests there in the Museu de Soares dos Reis.

Close by the Cathedral and, therefore, a more than usually pointed reminder of a faith long discarded, the so-called Temple of Diana raises fourteen elegant columns against a larger Gothic backcloth. It closely resembles in style the temple of similar title in Merida, being both hexastyle and peripteral. The base is 10 feet high, 48 feet wide and 80 feet long, and is least well preserved at the front, where the steps gave access from ground-level. The columns themselves, which attain a height of nearly 24 feet above the base, are of granite stone and are fluted: all but two retain their Corinthian capitals which are of white marble from Estremoz, with architrave above. At the two corners small sections of the surmounting frieze can be seen as well. A marble thumb has been found that belonged to a statue 12 or more feet high, and is the only piece left of the representation of the unknown deity to whom the temple was dedicated. Built in the second century A.D. the temple is thought to have suffered the first stages of destruction as early as the fourth century, probably by Christians anxious to remove paganism from their midst. Later, some time in the Middle Ages, what was left of the temple was built into the walls of a fortress with crenelated parapets and Gothic doors: with the decline of the effectiveness of such fortifications, it suffered the indignity of being used as an abbatoir and it was not until the middle of the nineteenth century that it was restored to the state in which it can be seen today.

After Evora the tale of Roman remains in Portugal is soon told. There are, however, very good specimens of private baths to be seen near Santiago do Cacem (Merobriga), near the Atlantic coast, directly west of Beja. A State inn stands near the site. Very nearly a complete plan of the baths can be identified—tepidarium, frigidarium and caldarium with subterranean hypocausts where appropriate: the entry of the water into the establishment and its subsequent distribution can also be traced. That the owner was a man of affluence may be deduced from the number of columns and capitals that adorned some of the chambers and from the fact that at least one room used to be faced with marble. The town of Santiago has a small museum with some interesting exhibits in the smaller range to reinforce the claims of this isolated part of Portugal upon the attention of Roman enthusiasts.

Of Pax Julia (Beja), the capital of a subdivision of Lusitania, no major feature has survived, unless we except the Porta de Evora, near the castle, which has a deal of work in it of recognisably Roman origin: small sections of Roman stonework may be seen in the present city walls. As is so often the case in Portugal, the local museum—here near the City Hall—in part makes amends, with its fine display of smaller items, for the disappearance of larger ones. Beja dominates a wide area of flat corn lands that are for Portugal what the Beauce is for France. It is not too fanciful to suppose that the agricultural scene of today does not differ in essentials from that upon which the Romans of the Early Empire looked. By way of contrast, however, about 30 kms. to the south-west near Aljustrel were the mines of Metallum Vipacense and in one of the waste-tips two bronze plaques were found containing rules for the day-to-day working of the mines. Both are now kept in Lisbon, one in the museum at Belem, previously mentioned, the other in the Museum of the Geological Commission.

Fifty-three kilometres south of Beja is the little walled town of Mertiola (Myrtilis), whose streets lead steeply down to the river Guadiana, whence protrude the broken stumps of a Roman bridge. Two larger-than-life marble statues, one representing a male, the other a woman, were unearthed at Mertiola: although headless and handless, they were taken to the museum at Belem and are to be seen there: a later find—the head of the Mother Goddess, Cybele—followed suit.

The lush, south-coast province of Algarve, whose

beauties have won at least a passing reference from the ancient poets from Homer to Avienus, inevitably attracted the Romans, and although some good archaeological work has been done, much more remains to be done. Indeed, the south coast and the district round Medobriga, north of Portalegre, promise the richest and most immediate yield of all Roman sites still to be explored. The best so far, first discovered as long ago as 1877, are the extensive baths found at Milreu, near the eighteenth-century palace of Estoi, 8 kms. north of the provincial capital Faro. It covered an area of nearly 6,000 square yards, and, quite apart from its impressive size, the *de luxe* nature of the amenities provided is revealed in the many fine mosaics which were found in abundance throughout the full range of the now-familiar apodyterium, caldarium, frigidarium, etc., duplicated to accommodate the two sexes separately. A recurrent motif in the mosaics is a fish, the symbol—almost the trade-mark—of Roman Ossonoba (Faro). Among the incidental discoveries here was a finely sculpted head of the Emperor Galienus, perhaps the finest piece of its kind yet found in the Peninsula, which is now kept in the museum at Lagos.

That Ossonoba had been a place of some consequence under the Romans is an accepted historical fact, if only because there was clear evidence that it had minted its own coinage and, in the late Empire, had been the seat of a bishopric, seven of the occupants of which were known by name. But for a long time there was doubt as to its precise location. After the discovery of the baths at Milreu, it was thought that it might lie between there and the village of Estoi. But recent investigations would appear conclusively to identify it with the modern town of Faro. The site

Temple of Diana at Evora

Amphitheatre at Italica

Arch at Cabanes

of a temple dedicated to Augustus was revealed in 1940 in the Cathedral square. Among the details unearthed was a plaque making reference to a certain priest of the town of Ossonoba. A Luso-Romano cemetery was exhumed in a suburb of the town called Letes: one of the sculptures from it has been carefully restored and is on view in the Faro museum, along with various stones, inscribed with references to Ossonoba, that have been taken from the wall that surrounds the old part of the town. Incidentally let it be said, if the name Faro suggests, phonetically at least, the existence of a Roman lighthouse, it is misleading, since it is of Moorish derivation.

Further west along the coast, at Abicada, near the small township of Figueira, between Portimão and Lagos, a Roman villa was located and excavated in 1938. It bore all the hall-marks of affluence—mosaics and frescoes and the like—that this well-favoured countryside would properly attract to itself. A section of the villa has been restored and transferred to the Museum at Lagos.

By way of contrast, to the east, some 25 kms. short of the Spanish frontier, the Roman Balsa still remains to be investigated: it is to be found near Tavira and lies under the fields of two farms that bear the significant titles of Torre de Ares and de Antas. It is said that to put a spade in the ground is to unearth dozens of fragments. Local tradition has it that Balsa was once possessed of a Roman circus. One hopes that this may some day be verified. For nothing is more striking in any study of Roman Portugal than the almost complete absence, up to date, of theatres, amphitheatres and circuses.

CHAPTER XIII

Baetica

ALTHOUGH the most thickly populated of the three Roman provinces, Baetica may be thought to be something of a disappointment as a source of Roman remains, in comparison with the other two. Inevitably in the course of fifteen hundred years, during which the centre of gravity of history has been moving westwards, any direct architectural link with Rome in the western provinces is a matter of bits and pieces as a rule. Tarraconensis was comparatively fortunate because at an early date Barcelona was selected for development, when Tarragona was the victim of some of the first barbarian raids in the third century. So the provincial capital was spared the further destruction which transformation into a modern city would have entailed. Lusitania was even more fortunate in the survival of its capital: with the result that both provinces have a focal point of interest for students of Rome. There is no such place in Baetica, at least not to the same degree, because Cordoba the capital was taken over by the Moors and, as has already been stated in the introductory remarks to Lusitania, the province consisted of an astonishing number of small communities, and provision for each and every one of those major amenities that by reason of their size are the hardest to obliterate, would have taxed the resources of even the Roman Empire.

However, Estremadura and South Portugal—to give them their modern names—were liberally supplied with baths—although, to correct possibly a false impression from such a remark, it must be stated that baths, particularly medicinal baths, did not lose their value just because the Romans were no longer concerned and, therefore, tended to survive for their own sakes. Be that as it may, Roman baths were found in 1893 in the ruins of Nertobriga, 2 kms. south-east of Fregenal de la Sierra, halfway along the Merida-Huelva road. They conformed closely to the conventional form: there was a hypocaust, with nine brick pillars standing 2 feet high and flues lined with brick and stone: above were the various rooms, some apsidal, arranged in two main sections divided by a gallery.

There are two further places of interest in the Province of Badajoz—both to the east of the Merida-Seville road. In Zalamea de la Serena there is obviously some Roman work incorporated in the lower levels of the church tower, a tall base and three columns, forming one angle: they are presumed to have been part of either a temple or monumental memorial in temple form. At Regina (Casas de Reina) there are the remnants of a Roman theatre, but in this instance rather unusual remnants. Here little or none of the terraces of seats are left, but the outside, semicircular wall with three doorways in it and, 17 feet inside it, a second concentric wall that once stood behind the pathway that separated the second ring of seats from the third. Most unusual of all is the front wall of the stage set-piece, with apertures, where once were fixed the three 'valvae' that gave access to the stage from the rear. Since the total diameter is not more than 175 feet, this must have been considered a small theatre in its day, but for size, it matches the one at Medellin.

If the fortunate visitor to Seville in Holy Week, or during the Feria that follows, is tempted to think that he is far removed from anything to do with Ancient Rome both in actuality and in spirit, he would be wrong in respect of the latter at least, for few peoples could compete with the Romans when it came to putting on a show, and if they liked to think that 'gravitas' was one of their main characteristics, that does not mean that they did not know how to relax.

But with regard to actuality, the point would be only too well made. For precious little is left of the city of Hispalis that cold-shouldered Julius Caesar before the battle of Munda almost exactly two thousand years ago. However, between the Puertas de la Macarena and de Cordoba there are 500 yards or so of Roman wall—although much restored by later Moorish and Christian hands—relieved by six rectangular towers: there is also an interior vaulted gallery. To the east of the city, an aqueduct, known as Caños de Carmona, brought water to Hispalis from Alcala de Guadaira some miles away. As it approached the city it emerged from under the ground on to a long double-arched structure made of brick. The pillars are 4 feet square and stand just over 7 feet apart and inevitably are marred by patches of later restoration.

For anything else, there is nothing more substantial than literary evidence: one hundred and twenty years ago, traces of a Roman theatre still existed in the Bocineguería, and as for temples, there is an inscriptional reference to one, and in the Calle de Marmoles some columns were found that may be related to it. However, the Roman researches of the casual visitor to Seville can never end in complete frustration so long as the Museo Arqueologico Provincial with its fine collection of smaller Roman pieces from Seville and Italica continues to be so magnificently housed in the Palacio de las Bellas Artes, a semicircular pavilion erected in the Parque de Maria Luisa for a recent Hispano-American Trade Fair.

But if, along with other large cities, Seville proves disappointing in the particular field to which this book is devoted, it quickly makes amends in its immediate neighbourhood: for 1 km. distant from Santiponce, itself only 6 kms. to the north-west of the city, lie the ruins of Italica, almost the very earliest Roman foundation in Spain, dating from 206 B.C. and the birthplace of at least two Roman Emperors. Here within traceable precincts is the most productive and rewarding Roman site of the whole province: private houses, baths, amphitheatre, streets and drains are here on view in varying stages of completeness. There are, in addition, hints of a theatre and a temple, representing, as it were, the many other fine buildings of which nothing at all has hitherto been found.

As in the finer cities of Italy, the streets were paved with large flag-stones, and many of the houses, as befitted a city of its reputation, were sumptuous and elegant. One such, at least, has been explored and a high degree of stylish planning was revealed within its rectangle of 40 yards by 24 yards. It does not compare for sheer size with the vast residence adjacent to the main gate of Conimbriga, but merits a brief description, if only for the unusual number of courts it possessed. The main door leads into the atrium, with galleries that gave, on the right, to the servants' quarters: to the left to the dining-room which had a mosaic floor, and straight across to the 'tablinum' (chief reception room). To right and left of this was a patio, one for the use of each sex, perhaps, and the rectangle is concluded in depth by an open peristyle, flanked by further rooms.

The baths were equally impressive: with regular dimensions of 80 yards by 68 yards, they were likely to have been the most extensive of any in the province. The façade, adorned by statuary, was on one of the two shorter sides and a portico ran the length of it, masking the approach to seven doorways. The three in the centre opened into an 'atrium' with a portico inset into two sides. The two pairs of doors at each end of the façade led into a similar series of chambers that were obviously intended for separate use by men and women. The men's premises were on the right and since they included most of the centre of the building as well, were designed to cope with larger numbers. The first room in each set of rooms was the dressing-room (apodyterium). This is followed in turn by two bath chambers that were probably 'caldarium' and 'tepidarium', because the hypocaust is definitely beyond these and must mark the site of the 'laconicum'. The 'frigidarium' was in the centre of the building and was approached by descending steps, while the rooms at the furthest end were used, in all probability, for massage.

The high quality of these amenities is reflected in a smaller bathing establishment, also severely rectangular, which can be seen at ground-level or slightly above. Here the façade had a central portico and four doors only. Behind, a 'vestibulum' led into a columnated patio and at the far end, beyond some small rooms was a large apsidal hall, which the presence in the floor of steps suggests was the setting for the 'frigidarium'. Here too, among the numerous smaller premises, there was ample scope for the segregation of the sexes.

In general, temples and theatres in Baetica have fared ill. But whereas the site of a temple in Seville is not decisively proved, better fortune attended excavations in Italica in the year 1900 when a temple of Diana was located, and the resultant finds bodily transferred to the Museum in Seville—a statue of Diana and two complete Corinthian columns, 14 feet high, and fragments of others, relics meagre enough in all conscience and barely worth recording, were it not that on the pedestal of the statue there is engraved a plan of the temple, showing the usual rectangular shape and the cella divided into three with an apsidal end, as in the Temple of Venus in Rome.

The theatre at Italica is even more a subject for conjecture and is thought to lie beneath a hollow not far from the amphitheatre, thus repeating the arrangement at Merida. However, the amphitheatre is important enough a monument in its own right, being the largest in the Peninsula and the fourth largest in the Roman world. With overall dimensions of 170 yards by 145 yards, it has about 30 yards' advantage over Merida in both directions. The site is on the north-west outskirts taking advantage of two suitable slopes, and was first excavated in 1860, with additional work in the course of the present century. The east gate was the main one and the road through it was paved. There was one door on each side of it which gave access to the front seats reserved for prominent members of the public and there was a similar arrangement at the opposite, west end, too. Ring galleries ran behind the lowest order of seating, interrupted halfway along each of the two sides by the retiring chamber built for the convenience of the distinguished personage occupying the tribunal above. Both rooms were undoubtedly finished off in some style—in each there is a niche that once held a piece of statuary—and were large enough for meals to be served in them.

The 'podium' or wall that marks the limits of the actual arena was faced with marble and stands about 7 feet high: originally there would be additional protection of ropework to protect the immediate spectators. Behind rose the eight rows of seats for the 'equites' and above them, separated by a flat passage-way, the eleven rows of the centre section. These were served by the aforementioned galleries beneath them: whereas the outer range of seats, amounting to twelve rows, were approached directly from the hillside through doors in the exterior wall of the amphitheatre. But it is in these upper ranges that the greatest depredations have taken place, and we have to rely on the description of the 1860 excavations for the number of rows of seats, for instance. But even so, there are still indications of a terrace at the top where awnings were rigged to provide welcome shade for spectators. The whole 'cavea' was split into sixteen 'cunei' or wedges by radiating and ascending stairways.

In the floor of the arena, the 'fossa' or underground section is visible. It is the same shape as that at Merida, comprising a central square with a rectangular gallery projecting from the two sides that face the end gates of the arena. Across the central square section, in line with the side walls of the projecting galleries were two lines of four pillars each, whose tops bore the marks of the beams that supported the floor of the arena. These underground premises, which were directly served by a drain or sewer, launched the wild beasts into the arena from their temporary cages and received in return their mangled bodies and those of their victims. It requires little imagination to realise that the drain was in no sense a superfluous amenity.

Nothing has been found that assigns a definite date to the construction of the amphitheatre, and, in the absence of conclusive evidence, it is commonly assigned to the Emperor Trajan, a native of the city. What has been found is a segment of a large bronze tablet recording the details of a senatorial decree passed at the instigation of the Emperor Marcus Aurelius (A.D. 161-180) regulating the cost of public presentations, the pay of the gladiators and the obligations to them of their employers.

The provincial town of Carmona (Carmo) stands on a ridge looking over the Andalusian plain to the Sierra Morena, 33 kms. along the road from Seville to Cordoba. Roman associations are not far to seek: for the Puerta de Sevilla, despite its unusual form, has a good deal of Roman work in it. The gate consists of a covered passage, divided into two sections by a kind of patio of irregular shape. It is here to the right of the patio that there is a small section of wall—some 4 feet by 2 feet—that is thought to date from the time of the Carthaginian wars in Spain at the end of the third century B.C. and therefore to be the earliest piece of Roman masonry in the Peninsula. The remainder of the Roman work in the gate is assigned to a date in the reign of Trajan. The two arches of the outer section are Roman, as is the intervening vaulting: the inner section, leading into the town, was fairly heavily restored by the Moors. This type of double defensive gateway is not Roman in origin, but Babylonian, and was adopted later by Greeks, Romans and Moors in descending order of frequency. The walls of Carmona are almost entirely reconstructions, at various dates, of the defences that Caesar noted, as the strongest in the whole of Hispania Ulterior. On the other hand, the Cordoba gate, which looks like a Roman gate to end all Roman gates, is a piece of hybrid restoration perpetrated in the seventeenth or eighteenth century.

The amphitheatre here has survived sufficiently to be definitely identified as one, but to little further purpose. The two entrances at the narrow ends of the ellipse can be seen and the arena itself can be measured as having been nearly 60 yards by 42 yards.

However, the extensive necropolis would always attract attention to Carmona even if there were no gate and no amphitheatre. Within an area of 1 km. to the west of the town some hundreds of tombs have been found, some in the form of inhumation, others, later ones, represented by the presence of cinerary urns. The most striking of the earlier tombs, which may date from as early as Republican times, is that of Postumius. Here a stairway descends into what was an open patio with an altar in one corner and in another a shallow channel in the floor for the pouring of libations. The actual sepulchral chamber which leads off from the patio in the opposite direction to the line of the stairs, is itself provided with a shallow 'fossa' too, and, at a later date, with seven niches for the receipt of cinerary urns. The walls are decorated with painted representations of birds and dolphins, executed by an artist who may have left his name—C. Silva(nus).

The commonest and simplest form of cinerary burial is in an underground crypt, with a flat or vaulted roof:

such crypts are generally reached by a square passage containing a stairway. Besides having niches, where urns may stand, the walls of the crypt are often decorated with pictures painted on the plaster, and in many instances the tombs have received names of identification in accordance with the subjects so illustrated. The tomb of the Funereal Banquet reproduces the traditional layout of the Roman dinner party by representing one couch and one table on each of three walls of the crypt. In the Tumba de la Paloma a dove is painted in the centre of the vaulted roof. Others are known by the name given on the actual urn, e.g. the Tumba de Prepusa. One crypt has an unusual architectural feature in the form of four pillars ranged round its centre: another tomb has three chambers with doors leading to right, left and centre at the foot of the stairway. On the other hand, the so-called Ustrinum not unexpectedly features a crematorium, which is found at the foot of a well-like shaft over 7 feet deep. The actual chamber leading from it is 6 feet deep, 5 feet long and nearly 3 feet wide, and from the calcinated condition of its walls had obviously been put, in its day, to plentiful use.

True to its name, the 'columbarium' is liberally supplied with niches, having two rows of them on three of the four walls that form quite a large square room. The floor space bounded by these three walls is largely occupied by stone seats and table in the normal setting of 'triclinium': near the fourth wall is an altar and a trough for libations. Another tomb, however, goes one better in this respect, or to be completely accurate, two better: for it has three 'triclinia'. At the foot of the stairway, on the right, is a niche that contained a representation of the Lares (household gods) and when an open patio is entered, on the right is one 'triclinium', open to the sun and, therefore, perhaps for use in winter: on the other side, a second set, under the shadow of a wall, and, if the bases of pillars mean anything, also under the shelter of an arbour. Presiding over this dining-room set, from a niche in the wall above, is the seated figure of a woman amply clad and with a vessel in her hand. A variety of subterranean chambers lead off from the patio: one contains the third set of stone chairs and table: a second is an improvised kitchen with a hole in the vaulted roof: and, in addition to accommodation for table utensils and for clothes, there is the tomb itself with seven niches in its walls. A small stone elephant that was found here, has, in the absence of any signs of ownership, rather incongruously lent its name to these elaborate premises.

Still more elaborate, however, was a later discovery, an extensive open patio with stone 'triclinium' in the centre and surrounded by galleries supported by Corinthian columns. But most surprising of all was an underground chamber of very irregular shape that led off from one of the galleries. With its heavily groined, domed roof it was strongly reminiscent of a burial chamber of the early Greek period, but it must in this setting be assigned to a Roman date. A further disconcerting fact was the failure to find in it any urn or similar object.

Another point of interest, although not in the immediate neighbourhood, but a few kilometres north near the river Guadalquivir, is the ancient town of Arva, near Alcolea del Rio, where among the general ruins, what had been considered to be the remains of an old foundry was found to have been a Roman bath. The 'frigidarium' was seen to have been lined with marble and to have been surrounded by a series of columns, also of marble. Adjoining was a semicircular construction and a brick-built conduit that connected with an aqueduct—now dilapidated—which fetched water from a spring called La Mezquita, 1 km. north of the town. But local tradition that insisted on there being some industrial remains was not far from the mark: for there were actually found the ruins of a small pottery factory whose walls seemed to have consisted of a curious jumble of broken pottery and stone, set between regular layers of broad bricks and the whole supported by pilasters or buttresses of cut stone. In one of the workshops the stand that once supported a potter's wheel was *in situ*, surrounded by large containers full of clay and jars of chalk. A stamp bearing the words 'Officina Rivema' was also found.

There are two notable tombs of Roman date at Osuna (Urso) which is 84 kms. along the road from Seville to Antequera, and the nearest township to the site of the battle of Munda. Both are on the same rather complicated pattern, being divided up into various rectangular or square sections, each with vaulted roof. Graves roughly shaped to fit the human body had been hewn in the floors and the walls were decorated with paintings of festoons and birds, so closely resembling those in the catacombs at Rome as to suggest that the burials were Christian.

Some distance to the north-east, in the fertile plain between Cordoba and Andújar there is an attractive small Roman bridge where the Roman road from Cordoba to Castulo (Cazlona) crossed the Rio Salado de Porcuna, a tributary of the Guadalquivir: the road itself, of course, bears no signs of its Roman origin now, but the arches and much of the intervening pillars, including the small flood-arches, are obviously Roman work. Part of the attraction of this modest bridge is the ease with which one may stop and inspect it.

For a city that was once the capital of a province, from a Roman point of view, Cordoba is frankly disappointing, certainly when compared with the other two capitals, Merida and Tarragona. The only definite link with Imperial Rome is to be seen in the considerable amount of Roman stonework in most of the supports of the sixteen-arch, pontoon-like bridge that brings in the road from the south. It is customary to assign the responsibility for the complete disappearance of all the architectural links to the Moors, whose capital this was. It is known, for instance, that the Mosque was built on the site of a temple of Janus and that much material from it went into the present building. But at least two items finally disappeared at a much later date. When the Casas Consistoriales and the cloister of the Convent of San Pablo were built in 1730, there was still evidence on the site of the presence of an amphitheatre: and as recently as 1830 the forum could be located in or near the Plaza Mayor, with attendant basilica and court-house (curia), the latter being a place of some magnificence, since a coloured marble stairway and a rich mosaic floor belonging to it were brought to light when the foundations for the Colegio de la Asunción were dug out.

If each of the three Spanish provinces can be said to feature a particular item amongst their relics of the Roman past—Tarraconensis her memorial arches, Lusitania her bridges—then there is no doubt that Baetica can claim distinction for the many fine specimens of

Roman burials within its borders: and just within the eastern boundary is a single tomb belonging to a 'familia Pompeia' at a point wide of the town of Baena, which is 43 kms. to the south-east of Cordoba: a narrow entrance leads to a chamber, 9 feet by 6 feet, with a vaulted roof. Instead of the customary niches for urns, there is a ledge running round the four walls and the urns were small and rectangular. Experts have given to it a date of the Augustan period.

The next two items in all probability involve poaching on the preserves of Tarraconensis, but since neither is of major importance and both are so far removed from their fellows in their own province, it seemed best to consider them here. The first comprises some commercial premises that were discovered in Sierra del Castillo de Locubin in the province of Jaen: they measured 50 feet by 13 feet and were divided into four rooms of unequal size: among the charred remains were found weights and measures together with a quantity of Imperial coins. Perhaps the establishment was a 'ponderarium' or official premises for weighing. The second was the discovery of Roman baths on a farm, the Cortijo del Ahorcado, 30 kms. south-east of Linares. They covered a fairly wide area and in the centre was an unusually well-preserved 'frigidarium', thought to have been open to the sky, but surrounded by a portico whose columns reflected an Iberian, pre-Roman style. Galleries led off from all round this central feature, those on one side in particular to four round rooms which housed individual warm baths.

The chief centres of Moorish occupation have so far proved largely barren of material for these pages, and Granada is no exception. The Alhambra reigns supreme and unchallenged. But it was not always so.

As comparatively recently as the eighteenth century the forum of the Roman community of Illiberis was visible, at least in part, near the Alcazaba, immediately to the west of the Alhambra: the stairway of a temple and a portico fronting a basilica, were there in support. Enquiries on the spot might possibly elicit the whereabouts of a plan, that is known to exist, of the Roman forum. Otherwise the only existing monument that the whole province of Granada has to offer is what is left of an aqueduct at Almuñecar on the coast—a single row of arches carrying a vaulted channel with ventilation towers at intervals.

Malaga's links with Roman Malaca are memories too: the site of a Roman amphitheatre was uncovered when the foundations of the Hospital of Santa Anna and of a nearby monastery were being laid. Very recent reports, however, mention that work on new premises for the Archaeological Museum in the lower part of the city behind the Alcazaba has revealed the outlines of a large Roman theatre. If this comes to anything, it will rival the only other monument the province of Malaga possesses, the little theatre at Ronda la Vieja (Acinipo) which lies 12 kms. to the north of Ronda and should not be confused with it. Here the bowl of the auditorium (cavea) is largely destroyed, but more of the stage setting and premises at the back (postscaena) has survived than in any other theatre in Spain. Built entirely of stone, there is the front wall of the stage set-piece (frons scaenae), with the three doors and part of the rear and side walls as well. Inside there are two storeys, including quarters for the actors: but of any portico or series of statues that may once have embellished the 'frons scaenae' no vestige remains: the two vaulted galleries of the main entrances, parallel to the stage and immediately adjoining it, can be seen: and even of the much mutilated 'cavea' eleven consecutive rows can be made out, split horizontally into eight and three by a concentric passage-way, and vertically into six sections by stairways. The comparative smallness of the theatre is revealed by the dimensions of the stage, 100 feet by 25 feet.

With the failure of Cadiz to retain anything from the time when it was 'jocosae Gades'—a failure which can to some extent be laid at the door of the English, for they figure more than once in the long list of raiders who have laid it waste—there remains but one centre to describe. That is the ruined site of Bolonia (Belo) on the coast west of Tarifa, facing Tangier. The most striking feature, revealed as the result of excavations in the early 'twenties, is a triple temple of Jupiter, Juno and Minerva. The separate 'cellae' stood each on its own pedestal 7 feet 6 inches high, complete with stairway on the front, and measured roughly 25 feet by 16 feet, except the one on the left, which was a little wider. In the interior of each cell was a ledge on the wall—apparently for statues, for a marble statue of a toga-clad person was found on the site; also fragments of a seated figure of Juno: stumps of altar stones were found in front of the 'cellae', on the terrace. As for columns, each temple was tetrastyle and pseudo-peripteral: i.e. some of the side columns were sunk into the walls of the 'cella' to give the effect of pilasters. The pillars were fluted only in the upper half and the capitals were a composite of Corinthian and Ionian orders.

Proof of the existence of other urban amenities was also forthcoming: a paved section of the forum, the ellipse of an amphitheatre and the remains of a small theatre that possessed an unusual feature: the whole of it had been an artificial construction and no attempt had been made to create appropriate contours in the ground. As for the rest, there was a semicircular outer wall with seven doorways and sufficient rows of seating to reveal eight 'cunei' formed by ascending stairways and at least one horizontal passage-way.

Of the dwelling-houses, particular attention was given to two, one on each side of the street, near the eastern gate of the town. Both were true to the now familiar pattern of a good-class residence of the late Empire period—columnated 'atrium' and peristyle with primary and secondary quarters built round: one house has rooms each side of the entrance from the street, that did not communicate with the interior and must therefore have been shops; a touch of originality is added to the other by the presence of a marble sundial. But unique is the word for the vast premises that were discovered hard up against the wall of the town. Belo had been established as a tunny-fishing centre by the Phoenicians along with other towns on the south coast—notably Malaga—and the Romans, whose upper levels of society were well-known for their protracted menus, went out of their way to build up a trade in exported fish. So these premises proved to have been used for the salting of fish. The available space had been divided into various departments and the majority of them had square tanks, fifteen in all, built into the floor, carefully cemented with rounded corners. Five departments had no tanks and were possibly used for the cleaning of the fish, while one adorned with columns may well have been a sale-room or a shop.

CHAPTER XIV

Spain's Contribution to Roman Life and Letters

THE title of this chapter should not be allowed to create a false impression. To the Romans the word Hispania was a geographical term denoting the whole peninsula south of the Pyrenees: it did not mean the separate national entity that the word Spain means today. More often than not in Latin literature 'Hispania' appears in the plural, referring to the varying number of provinces that were to be found there throughout the long history of Roman dominance. Furthermore, that dominance was expressed in such political terms that a national contribution in the sense that we understand the phrase, was impossible. It is not that local patriotism in the provinces was discouraged entirely, but that, owing to natural restrictions on transport and the virtual absence of the inter-communication of ideas, to mention only two contributing factors, it was to all intents and purposes confined to the community in which a person lived, and that community, for the vast majority of provincials under the Roman Empire, was a city or a town. Within that community talent was, no doubt, actively encouraged in order that life in it should not stagnate, but be recurrently refreshed from home-produced sources. There must have been instances in the fifth century, when the barbarians broke through permanently in the west, of Roman towns and cities surviving for a number of years in isolation, quite capable of maintaining their communal life in face of the desultory attacks of an enemy who had no more than a predatory interest in urban civilisation.

Between the local community and Rome, however, there was no halfway stage. There was no attempt at 'dominion' status. We can see now, after the event, that had the Peninsula enjoyed such a status, and had consequently been allowed to be enriched by the talents that were creamed off by Rome, with the aid of the Pyrenees it might have fended off the Visigoths and Vandals and so changed the course of European history. But rightly or wrongly, consciously or unconsciously, by the circumstances of geography, the Roman Empire was in effect a world government and we who are inching our way painfully towards that goal and in the process are creating additional nations in the hope of uniting them later, are in no position to reproach the Romans for not indulging in this somewhat illogical expedient.

It should, therefore, be readily apparent that for those in the Peninsula who had ambitions of any sort that took them beyond the bounds of their own community there was no alternative to Rome as a prospective breeding-ground for their talents. Consequently there were many of these who left their native land, won their place in history and never returned. But in any book on Roman Spain it is right and proper that they should receive mention and their meed of praise. At the lowest estimate, if a metaphor of school life may be used, they are 'Old Boys' who did well.

In so far as the persons who made the contribution

to Roman life in the field of the arts went to Rome to make it, it is not surprising that their work is indistinguishable from Roman art in general, and has little or no native quality in it. This assessment may come as a disappointment to those who remember the dynamic cave-drawings of Altamira or the pronounced individuality of Gallic art, but it does not imply that the pre-Roman population—the Celtiberi, Lusitani, Turdetani, etc.—had no art form of their own: it simply means that the additional years of subjection (200-50 B.C.) and the sustained policy of intense Romanisation have combined with the normal toll of time virtually to obliterate it. Even before the Romans arrived, the long Mediterranean coast of Spain was subjected directly to the influence of both the Greeks and the Carthaginians, who colonised it to a far greater degree than the south coast of France. The most famous art 'find' of the pre-Roman period, the Lady of Elche, a life-size sandstone sculpture now in the Prado in Madrid, is Greek both in conception and execution.

So although the Roman museums of Spain and Portugal contain collections of coins, sculptures, inscriptions, pottery and the like that are admirable specimens of their period there is little that reflects anything that can be described as a local characteristic. Where this is possible, it is natural that the piece or pieces concerned hailed from the remoter country districts. Sculptures from the mining district of Cazlona reveal an original combination of human and geometrical figures. Further north it has been observed that funeral 'stelae' (pillars) from Clunia (Coruña del Conde) and Palencia and from the Cantabrians and the Pyrenees proclaim a similar technique, that low-relief which is more usually associated with wood-carving. The museum at Guimaraes near Coimbra in Portugal has a good selection of Lusitanian pieces of the pre-Roman or early Roman period. Pottery was mainly modelled on Italian or Gallic lines. Only Saguntine vases established an identity for themselves, being solid and durable, and were exported in some quantity to Rome. They were usually either cream-coloured or glazed red and often had potters' marks on them in the shape of a bee, a butterfly or a rabbit.

Literature, as an art form in the context of this chapter, has fared much better. Here the contribution was massive and a large proportion of so-called Silver Latin is the work of Spanish-born authors. During the golden age of the language, whose end coincided with the death of Augustus in A.D. 14, it was Italy that made the vital contribution in the persons of Cicero, Virgil, Horace and Livy. Ovid with his ability, as it were, to dash off either a hymn or an advertisement in elegiacs, is an appropriate link in style as he is in time between the two literary eras. For it is recognised that the post-Augustan writers came to prefer smartness and a kind of artificial brilliance to the rounded harmonies of their immediate predecessors.

With rhetoric and declamation playing so large a part in Roman education, it was well-nigh inevitable that writing should fall into the error of straining after effect, and degenerate into something akin to the journalism of our own time. It was essentially the age of the well-turned phrase, the heyday of the epigram.

Literary standards were therefore already declining before the provinces outside Italy had reached that stage in their development which enabled them to make an effective contribution. If a little over-simplification be permitted, these contributions were made—and it is not only in literature that this applies, but to some extent also in the political sphere—separately, century by century. Spain's influence was predominant in the first century A.D., Africa's in the second, and Gaul's in the third.

First of the Spaniards was the elder Seneca, who was born into a family of the business community of Cordoba round about the year 55 B.C. In the course of a very long life—he was over ninety years of age when he died—he made his mark as a rhetorician. His early education he received in Cordoba, since the Civil Wars prevented his going to Rome. He arrived in the capital some time after Cicero's death (43 B.C.) and he became a student under a fellow Spaniard, Marullus. Later he returned to Cordoba, perhaps with an official appointment on the provincial staff, and there married Helvia, a woman of good family, whose cultural interests in philosophy matched his own achievements as a rhetorician. She was to prove a decisive influence over the most talented of the three sons born to them.

By A.D. 4 Seneca was once more in Rome where he spent the remaining years of his long life. His major works—the *Suasoriae*, essays written in a deliberative style, and the *Controversiae*, a collection of difficult legal cases—were the product of his later years. Apart from their general interest in revealing information about rhetorical training, which was so large a part of the education of the day, they reveal also the man himself, retired administrator turned scholar, stern critic of his times, and, like the great Cato of the past, whom he admired and in so many ways resembled, a stout champion of Rome against the claims of 'arrogant Greece'.

By way of contrast with his father, the younger Seneca never returned to his native Spain once he had left it for Rome, quite early in his childhood. Born in Cordoba in 4 B.C., he was destined to become more famous than his father, whose names he bore. After the normal education of a well-to-do Roman under a grammaticus and a rhetorician, he travelled fairly extensively, getting as far afield as Egypt on a visit to an aunt who was married to the governor of that province. It was through her kind offices that, on his return to Rome at about the age of thirty-five, he was able to begin a political career, combined with active legal work in the courts. By degrees, however, he began to turn more and more to literature and philosophy, but, becoming involved in the Imperial Court, he suffered a period of banishment on the island of Corsica from A.D. 41 to 49. Amongst the many writings of this period, he took occasion to note some similarities between the islanders and certain Spanish tribes and in one rather artless little poem bade Cordoba mourn for her exiled poet.

In A.D. 49, however, he was recalled to Rome to a praetorship, and his literary reputation was now such that he was appointed as tutor to the youthful Nero, surely one of the ill-starred appointments of history. It should not be forgotten, however, that the first five years of Nero's reign, under Seneca's statesmanlike influence, were good years and were later praised by the Emperor Trajan himself, but the good start was not maintained and soon the Emperor's many infamies made the position of his philosopher-guide increasingly difficult, with the result that in A.D. 62 Seneca forsook his wealth and his excellent position and passed into studious retirement. Many of his major philosophical works are ascribed to these last few years. But the time left to him was tragically short. It was sufficient merely for his name to be mentioned as the prospective new Emperor in connection with the conspiracy of Piso in A.D. 65 to ensure the passing of the death sentence upon him. Tacitus has left us a moving account of the final scene, in which it is clear Seneca achieved the dignity, courage and pathos of a Socrates.

The comparison with Socrates is apt in one other respect. As a philosopher, Seneca was an orthodox Stoic and displayed no great originality or powers of penetrative thought. But like Socrates he did reject the anthropomorphic theology of his day and it is this aspect of his philosophical works that made him perhaps the most popular of pagan philosophers with the early Christians. This popularity extended also to his play-writing and had odd consequences of a far-reaching nature. The plays themselves were little more than transcriptions of themes that Euripides had used, e.g. Hercules, Troades, Phoenissae, Medea, etc., and can never have been intended for performance on a stage, but only for recitation or declamation in private circles so effectively had the art of the 'pantomimus' ousted tragedy from the stage. While they are uniformly clever, and have occasional passages of some distinction, for us their main innovation is the author's manifest desire to make the flesh creep by his insistence in gory details. This has been taken by modern Spanish historians to be a markedly Spanish trait: and so it is. But thanks to the affinity previously mentioned between the Church and Seneca, the violence that marks some of the scenes of our own Elizabethan dramatists is in direct line of succession to it.

A third member of the Seneca family, Lucan, nephew

of the philospher, had even less of a direct connection with Spain, for he was taken from Cordoba to Rome only a few weeks after his birth in A.D. 39. A young life of considerable literary promise was cut short when he was implicated along with his uncle in the Pisonian conspiracy of A.D. 65. Before he was twenty years old he was enjoying the favours of the Emperor and his first public literary success was his *Laudes Neronis* in the year A.D. 60. But his position declined with that of his uncle and he embarked upon the ten books of the work most closely associated with his name, the *Pharsalia*. This was a study in verse of the Civil War of more than one hundred years before and, although it has been described as an epic without a hero, it obviously favoured the Senate in its opposition to Julius Caesar. Such a topic with such an attitude amounted, under Nero, to an act of great political courage, if not open defiance. The fourth book describes Caesar's campaign near Lerida, but it is obvious that to the author, Spain was just another country. The artificiality of his style is fittingly revealed in a lengthy description, extending over several hundreds of lines, of a sea battle. The simple word 'navis' is studiously avoided throughout.

The Romans were curiously neglectful of geography, a study of which would have been so useful to them both in their administration of conquered lands and in their invasions of new ones. For instance, at the time of the conquest of Britain their knowledge of the island is not known to have been advanced beyond the information contained in the works of Pytheas of Marseilles, compiled in the fourth century B.C., except for the remarks on the subject made in Caesar's Commentaries. Spain supplied the first geographer to write in

Latin in the person of Pomponius Mela, a native of Tingentera, near Gibraltar. In the early forties of the first century A.D. he produced three geographical books in which, starting in Africa from the Pillars of Hercules, he surveys the shores of the Mediterranean and the Atlantic coastline of western Europe. Obviously under this arrangement the Spanish Peninsula receives extra attention and it may have been in accord with his natural sentiments that it should. The work is in no sense scientific even by the standards of his day, but his Herodotean digressions lend colour to it and from time to time he produces perspicacious comment. On the subject of Spain he has practically nothing to add to his Greek predecessor, Strabo. But he does realise that the Cantabrian mountains are in line with the Pyrenees and are virtually a continuation of them.

For writers on the fringe of Classical Latin and Greek there are vogues, even if they are not so pronounced as in the world of fashion and there are signs that the *De Re Rustica* of Columella is about to enjoy a period of favour. It could well be argued that appreciation of its merits is long overdue. The style of writing is clear and the nature of the subject matter in itself is a guarantee that the literary innovations and rhetorical devices that mar contemporary literature, are largely absent. The twelve books, into which the work is divided, adequately cover the whole range of agricultural activities, dealing, amongst other things, with the staffing of a farm, treatment of land, fruit trees, vineyards, poultry and fishponds and even the domestic duties of a farmer's wife. The tenth book—on gardening—is written in verse as a tribute to the *Georgics* of Virgil. Columella is unusually open in acknowledging the sources of his information, but he was not without knowledge and experience on his own account: for he was brought up near his native Cadiz, in the latter years of Augustus's reign, on the estate of his uncle who was, himself, a practical farmer of some renown. It cannot be claimed, however, that Columella's work has any direct connection with Spain. Much rather is it dedicated to the task of restoring agriculture to its rightful place of pre-eminence in the economy of the Empire. It was written in Italy during the time of Nero: after serving in the Roman army in Syria, Columella had acquired estates near Rome, where he moved in high society, claiming Seneca among his acquaintances.

All the distinguished 'alumni' of Spain that have so far been mentioned have hailed from the province of Baetica, and the almost complete failure on the part of the most sympathetic critics to distinguish any trace of native character in their works is further proof, if proof is necessary, of the high degree of Romanisation which the south of Spain had assimilated. When we come to consider the careers and achievements of Quintilian and Martial, as we do now, the search for characteristics that are essentially Spanish, will, in some small measure, be rewarded. Both were natives of the north and in Spain, as in other countries of Western Europe, climate and geography have combined to create differences between north and south, even inside one nation. The same factors were present then and there can be little doubt that they tended to produce the same effect.

In the first place, both Quintilian and Martial were obviously much more conscious of Spain as their home than their counterparts from Baetica would appear to have been. Quintilian returned to his native Calahorra

(Calagurris) in the upper reaches of the Ebro valley, where he had been born in the year A.D. 35, and there practised law for a number of years until he attracted the attention of Galba, the governor of his province, and was brought to Rome in A.D. 68 by him. It was in Rome that he had received his education as a youth, and his prospects at the end of it cannot, in the light of his eventual success, have been so poor as to induce him to return to a distant provincial town of comparative unimportance, if the decision to do so had not been reinforced by some degree of sentiment. Be that as it may, now that he was back in the capital for a second time, his success was swift and spectacular. He embarked on a career of teaching and in his capacity as a professor of rhetoric was subsidised directly by Vespasian and was thus the first European to receive state recognition as a teacher. For among his pupils he counted the younger Pliny and Tacitus, and when Domitian came to the throne he was appointed tutor to his household. The *Institutio Oratoria*, which alone of his literary works survived him, was written in the few short years of retirement that preceded his death in A.D. 95. It ends with his famous 'critique' of Roman authors, from which it may be of interest here to give his opinion of his fellow Spaniards. As a confirmed Ciceronian, he was unable to commend either Seneca or Lucan. Senecan eloquence he found corrupt and the more dangerous in that it was full of attractive faults: Lucan he roundly declared to be more a rhetorician than a poet. His powers of shrewd observation and his sense of vocation have been considered to be more typical of the modern Aragonese than of the ancient Romans. So too, surely, is the dignity he achieves when in the preface to the sixth book he records the loss of his second son in addition to that of his young wife and an earlier child.

Marcus Valerius Martialis, known to us as Martial, owes his third name not to any deeds of war on the part of himself or his ancestors, but simply to the fact that he was born on the first of March: in which year cannot be established, except that it was between A.D. 38 and 41. But the place was Bilbilis (Catalayud) and it was here he tells us that he received the best education that his parents were able to procure. He left home to go to Rome in A.D. 64 and for a brief year enjoyed the patronage of his compatriots, the younger Seneca and Lucan. It was not an auspicious start and he spent the next fifteen years of his life in complete obscurity. But his subsequent works make it clear that during that time he had lived a bohemian kind of life in which he made acquaintances in the highest levels of society and the lowest. The first of his known works was published in A.D. 80 under the title of *Liber Spectaculorum*, commemorating the opening of the Colosseum in that year by the Emperor Titus. The more famous *Epigrams* followed, roughly one book per year during the period A.D. 86-98.

As a writer, Martial has none of the scholarship or deeper seriousness of a Quintilian: he was a spectator upon life, the gifted reporter whose facility to coin a telling phrase raised the epigram almost to the level of an art. Despite more than thirty years of living in the sophisticated atmosphere of a capital city, he remained at heart very much the country boy—nowhere more so than in his hatred of sham and his complete self-revelation. He had no use for the mythological background that was traditional for Latin verse, but wrote simply of life as he saw it, for good or ill. The latter category may explain the Rabelaisian quality of a considerable proportion of his work, but it can hardly excuse it: for the two books of Epigrams dedicated to the Emperor Domitian are entirely free of pornography, thereby suggesting that the poet was not without standards of propriety. But even when he is at fault in this respect and in his fawning upon the great, he does not deny that he writes to please.

No author so readily, even in translation, takes his reader back to life in ancient Rome. But nevertheless it was a way of life of which, in the end, he sickened. With a change of emperors in A.D. 98, perhaps instinctively aware that the new régime would require adjustments which he was unwilling or unable to make, he returned to his native Bilbilis, where, thanks to the generosity of a patroness, he enjoyed the amenities of a small estate. The twelfth and final book of *Epigrams* followed after an interval of three years and cannot long have preceded his death. In it he reveals frequent glimpses of life in rural Spain in his day. He appreciated the privilege of sleeping late in a morning after more than thirty years of early rising in Rome: he watched the bailiff issuing rations to his staff: he noted the pots on the log fire, the shadows of the interlacing vines, the whitewashed dovecote and the tame eel in the pond. He loved the way the people of the pueblo danced when the festivals came round. 'You'll find no toga here', he wrote; 'if you ask for one, they will give you the rug from some broken-down chair.' Conventional words for a conventional scene, it may be objected. But it would run counter to all that we know of their author to imagine that they were not true. Indeed, in the same breath, he is not unaware of the disadvantages—no libraries, no good conversation, but only parochial gossip. But all in all, he tells us, that was how he chose to live and how he hoped to die, and it would seem that his hope was fulfilled.

By an odd coincidence, the year that marked the drying up of the flow of literature from Spanish sources with the passing of Martial from the Roman scene, was the very year in which the first man of Spanish birth ascended the imperial throne, in the person of Marcus Ulpius Trajanus. Under him the Empire reached its widest limits. But more relevant to this book than his campaigns in Transylvania and the Middle East are the circumstances that brought him, the first of the provincials, to his high office. He had been born in September A.D. 52 in Italica near Seville to a family of direct Italian descent, whose ancestor had been one of the veterans of Scipio concerned in the original foundation of the city almost exactly two hundred and fifty years before. His father, Marcus Ulpius Trajanus, was already embarked upon a political career that culminated in the governorship of his home province of Baetica under Vespasian.

From the start it is plain that the son had no other career in mind than the Army, and he saw service in it in many parts of the Empire. He was without political ambition, which often went hand in hand with an Army career: he was quite content to serve for ten years at the comparatively humble level of a military tribune. However, by the time the Emperor Nerva was casting round to find himself a successor, Trajan was commanding the Roman forces on the Rhine. Nerva himself had been appointed emperor in A.D. 96 when sixty-six years old, his safe age and his family connection with Julio-Claudian dynasty of the Augustus-Nero period being ample qualifications for what was patently a stop-gap appointment after the violent death of the unlamented Domitian, last of the Flavians. When very shortly afterwards the prospect of a strong successor was required to bolster the régime, the appointment of Trajan as political heir-apparent was greeted with almost universal approval, and only the most die-hard of constitutional purists found a regrettable precedent in this elevation of a provincial to the highest office of the State.

Note has been taken elsewhere in earlier chapters of the many practical developments that took place in Spain during the nineteen years of Trajan's reign. But it should be emphasised that these were but part of a widespread distribution of additional amenities throughout the Empire. Yet natural sentiments do honour even to the most exalted of men and it would be strange if Trajan felt no touch of pleasure or pride at being in a position to bestow such benefactions upon the land of his birth, and when the time came for him in his turn to look for a successor, it must have given him equal gratification to find one so well qualified, not merely in the ranks of his own countrymen, but within his own family circle.

One of the parents of Publius Aelius Hadrianus—it is not known which—was a cousin of Trajan; an ancestor of the father, had migrated from Hadria near the Adriatic in Italy to Italica at the time of its original settlement and the name of the mother, Domitia Paulina, who came from Cadiz, proclaims an equally close attachment to Roman or Italian stock. The youthful Hadrian lost both of his parents shortly after his birth and he owed his introduction to Greek education in Rome to his Uncle Trajan, who was himself childless. His fourteenth and fifteenth years he spent back in Italica, but in A.D. 93 he was again summoned to Rome to begin a military career, and in A.D. 98, on the accession of Trajan, he joined the Emperor's personal staff. He took part in both the Dacian Wars, rising, by the time of the Parthian campaign, to the position of chief of the Emperor's staff. There can be little doubt that Trajan had every intention that Hadrian should succeed him, but, with a reluctance, not uncommon in the physically robust, to make preparation for death, he almost left the proclamation too late. For it was only in the obscurity of a small town on the coast of Cilicia, where he was suddenly struck down by a fatal illness on his return journey from Parthia in the late summer of A.D. 117 that, two days before he died, he contrived to make the adoption of his nephew official. Had Hadrian not been generally acceptable, the shabby circumstances that surrounded his adoption would have sufficed to secure his rejection.

The adoption as successor of the best man for the job, even if he was a member of the Emperor's family, was a reversal of emphasis in an arrangement that had already produced two family dynasties, separated by the single catastrophic year of A.D. 69. The change in selection produced four successive Emperors, over a period of eighty years, whose efficient rule derived from many diverse qualities, but from none more welcome than a wholesome display of common sense. The last of the four was Marcus Aurelius (A.D. 161-180) who was born in Rome in A.D. 121 to a member of the family of the Annii, whose home was in Uccubi (Espejo) in the south of Spain. But this flimsy connection is only worthy of mention in this context to show how the flow of talent from Spain to Rome had dwindled to an insignificant trickle that history had ceased to record.

Much later, however, in A.D. 256 there was born in Cordoba one who not only rose to the high and, possibly, decisive position of religious adviser to Constantine the Great, but also performed the astonishing feat of living to be a hundred years old. For nearly fifty of these he was, as Bishop of Cordoba, the foremost bishop of his time and was held in universally high esteem. Considering his eminence, it is remarkable how little is known of his personal history. He is first mentioned as second in the list of bishops attending the Synod of Elvira (Granada) in A.D. 300. He himself stated on another occasion that he had been the victim of religious persecution, and from the terms of his reference this is not thought to have occurred during the major persecutions instituted by Diocletian, but a little earlier, about the year A.D. 292. Since the higher officers of the Church were usually the first to suffer in any outbreak of persecution, it is very likely that Hosius was already Bishop of Cordoba at the time.

His absence from the Synod of Arles in August A.D. 314, the most comprehensive of the councils of the Church so far held, can only be explained by the supposition that he was in attendance upon the Emperor Constantine during his campaign in Pannonia. Certainly there is evidence that he was attached to the imperial court in A.D. 316 and when by A.D. 323 Constantine, now master of an undivided Empire, sought to achieve religious concord within it, it was Hosius to whom he entrusted the delicate mission of visiting Bishop Arius in Alexandria, whose views on the Trinity were unorthodox, not to say heretical. The assignment was not an easy one—for instance, Hosius spoke no Greek—and when it failed, the Emperor decided to summon a council of the Church, and the Synod of Nicaea in Asia Minor was the outcome. At this conference the Emperor's own contribution to the proceedings was such as to make it clear that he had been well briefed by Hosius, but the latter's influence did not long survive it. Shortly after, when his master had been converted to the same Arian doctrines that he had once sought to destroy, Hosius returned to the comparative seclusion of his own diocese at Cordoba. He never saw Constantine again, for he did not emerge from his semi-retirement until A.D. 345, when, almost ninety years of age, he presided with undiminished vigour over the Council of Sardica.

Nor was this the end, although he would have died a happier man had it been so. With the conversion of Constantine to its precepts, Arianism had grown apace and under Constantius would not rest until Hosius, the staunchest supporter of the Nicene faith, had been brought to heel. In A.D. 355 Hosius was summoned by the Emperor to Milan, and overtures made to him were scornfully rejected. A whole year of cruel detention in Sirmio in Italy followed, and at the end of it, weighed down by his years and broken in spirit, Hosius made sufficient concessions to give his enemies their propaganda triumph. He may even have succumbed to the violence used against him and died at Sirmio in A.D. 357. A happier account, however, relates that he was allowed to end his days in Spain and even that, before his death, he recanted and was readmitted to the Catholic Church. But, in either event, the shadow cast upon his name at the end should not be allowed to obscure the honour due to him for the otherwise unblemished virtue of a long life.

Spain, however, was not destined to get through entirely free from the taint of heresy, of which Arianism had been one of the more violent forms. Those who deviated only by the undue emphasis which they laid upon a particular item of 'gnosis' or 'knowledge', were grouped under the general title of 'Gnostics'. Priscillianism, which gained some vogue in Spain and Southern Gaul in the late fourth century, was one such deviation. Unfortunately, but somewhat naturally, the opponents of these minor heresies were more inclined to set labels upon them than to explain their nature, and often what the heretics had to say for themselves has been suppressed; and this is the case with Priscillianism.

But of Priscillian himself, there is no doubt that he was a Spaniard of good family who sponsored this particular form of Gnosticism, on its introduction from Memphis in Egypt, so ardently that he quickly converted two bishops of southern Spain to the sect that bore his name. Under their hands, as an act of defiance to the Synod of Saragossa which in A.D. 380 condemned the movement, Priscillianus was consecrated Bishop of Avila. The bishops, now three in number, journeyed to Rome to appeal over the heads of their orthodox colleagues to the Spanish-born Pope Damasus. The tie of common birthplace availed them nothing, however, and they were rebuffed, and when, later, they appealed to Maximus, the would-be Emperor of the West, yet another Spaniard, it availed them still less. For the latter, anxious to rally orthodox opinion behind him, condemned Priscillian to death and banished the others to the Scilly Isles. But the strength of the support that Priscillianus enjoyed is revealed by the fact that elements of his sect lingered on and were still the subject of angry diatribes as late as the Council of Toledo in A.D. 447.

By the middle of the fourth century the Christian Church had been established as the official religion of the whole Empire for more than one hundred years, and felt secure enough to indulge in the luxury of treating those of its members who got out of step as a greater threat to its own existence than those who stood outside its ranks altogether. Consequently, a revival of interest in, and appreciation of, the best Roman authors of the pagan past was not any longer considered incompatible with the highest standards of Christian behaviour: and if the honour of providing the leading figure in this revival fell to Spain, what other province of Rome could more appropriately pay this final, retrospective tribute?

Aurelius Clemens Prudentius was born in A.D. 348 in the north of Spain, perhaps in Saragossa, to a Christian family of good standing. He received a traditional education in rhetoric and law and despite some youthful misdemeanours, to which he was later at some pains to confess, he received two important civil appointments in the province, and eventually a position of some importance in the Emperor's court. But apart from the excursion to Rome that this last involved, his life was spent in Spain. His extant poems were written fairly late in his not very long life and, while possessed of considerable literary merit, are remarkable chiefly for their variety. Both his lyrical and his hexameter poems are closely patterned on their classical counterparts of Horace, Virgil and Lucretius. In the former, he expresses the hope that he may be looked upon as a Christian Pindar who found his inspiration, not in the Olympic palms, but in the lives and deaths of Christian martyrs. These were not far to seek. Half of those who are honoured are found in his own native church of Spain and include Fructuosus of Tarragona and Eulalia of Merida. The rest are those whom he found specially honoured at Rome or on his journey thither.

The strictly classical style that Prudentius so successfully achieved was far removed from the poetic idiom of his own day, in which quantity was fast giving way to stress. The practice of singing hymns originally introduced into the west by St. Hilary of Poitiers in A.D. 360 had been gaining wide favour ever since, and was only rendered possible by the adoption of the new-style verse. In composing twelve hymns therefore for the various hours of the day in the old-fashioned quantitative style, which permitted only of a recitative performance, Prudentius may thereby be regarded as not very typical of his race. For in Spain, of all countries, poetry has come to be associated with instrumental accompaniment.

The rest of his poems are in hexameter verse: they deal with a variety of subjects ranging from the Deification of Man in Christ to a treatise on the Origin of Sin. His *Libri contra Symmachum* put the case against a revival of paganism that was being debated in high places at the turn of the century, but with no trace of fanaticism or even of that impersonal intellectualism, which is concerned only with dogma. Indeed, the religious feeling displayed throughout all his work is born of instinct rather than intellect and is much more closely akin to the feelings of the masses than the dictates of the hierarchy.

It is tempting to suppose that he is also the *vox populi* to the same extent when he expresses his great pride and pleasure at being a Roman. In Rome's past conquests and in her capacity for government he saw a preparation for the Kingdom of Christ, and he looked for greater conquests still under the banner of the Cross. His literary work was finished by A.D. 405 and he himself died shortly afterwards. In A.D. 409 the Vandals, the Suevi and the Alans, followed shortly by the Visigoths, swarmed through the Pyrenees and, overrunning the Peninsula, brought the political power of Rome therein to an end. Prudentius may, or may not, in the circumstances of his time, have been aware of the impending cataclysm, of which he became, possibly, one of the first victims. But at least it is dramatically satisfying that the last literary reference made by a native of Roman Spain to the power that had ruled it for so long should be a tribute. On balance, no doubt, it was deserved.

Appendix

THE ROMAN EMPERORS FROM AUGUSTUS TO HONORIUS

Augustus	27 B.C.-A.D. 14
Tiberius	A.D. 14-37
Caligula	37-41
Claudius	41-54
Nero	54-68
Galba	68-69
Otho	69
Vitellius	69
Vespasian	69-79
Titus	79-81
Domitian	81-96
Nerva	96-98
Trajan	98-117
Hadrian	117-138
Antoninus Pius	138-161
M. Aurelius	161-180
L. Verus	161-169
Commodus	180-193
Pertinax	193
Didius Iulianus	193
Septimius Severus	193-211
Caracalla	211-217
Geta	211-212
Macrinus	217-218
Elagabalus	218-222
Severus Alexander	222-235
Maximinus	238
Gordian I	238
Gordian II	238
Balbinus	238
Pupienus	238
Gordian III	238-244
Philip	244-249
Decius	249-251
Trebonianus	251-253
Aemilianus	253
Valerianus	253-260
Gallienus	253-268
Claudius Gothicus	268-270
Aurelian	270-275
Tacitus	275-276
Florianus	276
Probus	276-282
Carus	282-283
Carinus	283-285
Numerianus	283-284
Diocletian	284-305
Maximian	286-305
Constantius	292-306
Galerius	293-311
Licinius	311-323
Constantine	306-337
Constantine II	337-340
Constans	337-350
Constantius	337-361
Julian	361-363
Jovian	363-364
Valentinian	364-375
Valens	364-378
Gratian	375-383
Theodosius	379-395
Arcadius	395-408
Honorius	395-423

Overlapping dates refer to periods when co-partnership was in vogue.

Index